The Healing Journey:

Manual

For

A Grief Support Group

Anne C. Grant, Ph.D.

Vista publishing, Inc.

Edited by Jerena Burdge-Rezvan

Cover Design by Barry Power

Cover production supported by Thomas Taylor of ThomCatt Graphics

Vista Publishing, Inc.
473 Broadway
Long Branch, NJ 07740
(908) 229-6500

This publication is designed for use by facilitators of Grief Support Groups. All attempts have been exhausted by the author to obtain appropriate permissions for the works included in this publication. All acknowledgments, including "unknown" have been cited within the text.

Printed and bound in the United States of America

First Edition

ISBN: 1-880254-12-3
Library of Congress Catalog Card Number: 93-61852

U.S.A Price $24.95
Canada Price $31.95

DEDICATION

Dedicated to the hundreds with whom I've shared the healing journey.

MEET THE AUTHOR

Dr. Anne Grant's "mid-life transition," which she eventually came to understand as representing a "psychological death," with ensuing changes, and her 14 years in an acute care hospital Intensive Care Unit both played parts in her choice to work with dying patients and their families. Since Hospice is the only health care field where the patient *and* family are the therapeutic unit of care, that became her goal and she needed academic credibility of a Ph.D. in counseling psychology, via return to graduate school.

Dr. Grant has worked, now, for almost 10 years in the hospice field in varying capacities. She has acted as Social Service Counselor in both in-patient and at-home settings, Education Director, and, in more recent times, as Bereavement Coordinator, becoming ever more knowledgeable and specialized in the Grief & Loss field. It was as Social Service Counselor, in 1983, that she first began to facilitate groups.

She maintains a private practice for individuals, couples and families, and facilitates various kinds of groups. Since 1988, she has provided Grief Support Groups for "Kairos: Support for Caregivers" in San Francisco, and currently does four per week there, as well as a Family Drop-In Group twice a month. She facilitates two agency support groups. She also enjoys participating as a lecturer, on "Loss, Grief and Transition," both locally and for national conferences.

Dr. Grant lives in San Francisco and is fortunate to have her four adult children, with their families, living close by.

AUTHOR'S NOTE

Grief is a transition, a way to get from "here" (the loss) to "there" (the healing). Although this Manual is designed specifically for a Grief Group supporting loss via death, our grieving skills are challenged by *any kind* of loss: moving, ending of a relationship, retirement, a co-worker leaving. In my years of experience with grievers, I find that most of us have had neither teaching nor role models for *effective grieving,* so since we have no way to create a "map," our only choices become suppression, distraction or "over-ride." I find that once people face a loss traumatic enough to bring them to a Grief Support Group, all the previous life-losses come up underneath the current one. Many of us are restricted in our "acceptable" expression of feelings. Since grieving is *about feelings,* our mental capacity alone is inadequate. Time, without the work of grieving, is not enough: it just dulls the pain, and doesn't dissipate or resolve it. We are never able to reconcile the loss and move on, in charge, engaged in our lives.

Over the years I have received many calls from people wanting help to create a Grief Support Group. Writing this book seemed to be the best, most useful way to share this material. For my personal use, I have also compiled the "hand-outs" into a separate "Resource Book" and this broad spectrum material would be helpful to anyone who is grieving.

I wish you success in the use of this Manual to help those in need of your understanding support.

For those wishing to contact Dr. Grant directly, please write to her at:

Anne C. Grant, Ph.D.
5535 Anza
San Francisco, CA 94121

CONTENTS

Objectives of a Grief Support Group are to:

- create an emotional environment of caring, thus a "safe," trustable place to expose vulnerability

- facilitate a bonded group for mutual understanding and support

- balance between education and participation, passive/active

- validate the uniqueness of process and time frame

Goals for the participants of Grief Support Group:

- "Safe," trustable, supportive environment

- Decreased isolation, expanded support network with other group members

- Normalized "continuum of grief process"

- Opportunity to explore and articulate feelings/thoughts

- Expanded repertoire of coping skills

- For each, a unique "map" through the "territory" of grief

Introduction

You will certainly want to adapt the following information to your own need. Each group is different, even each session, and each requires a "dance" through the material, depending on the composition and immediate emotional needs of the group. Sometimes, for example, the group needs extra process time, so some of the "content" can be deleted or decreased. Other times, an issue arises in a session which lends itself to material from another session and can be "imported," then covered in more detail in the scheduled session. Use examples from your own experience to enrich and expand.

For each session there is more material than can be accommodated in the two hours. Choose according to your personal style. The size of the group creates varying demands. A group of 10, for example, takes longer for check-in, exercises and sharing than for a smaller group. Select among the "content" items to keep balances between: (1) thinking/feeling and (2) content/group sharing/ experiential exercise. Rely on hand-outs for the people who need/want more content than time allows.

Following each Session outline is material for (1) the facilitator's information or use and (2) material for "hand-outs" for the participants. The "hand-outs" can be Xeroxed and distributed for each session or can be compiled into a book and sold at cost in the first Session.

Remember that grief is *about* feelings; you are speaking *always* to their feelings: unlocking, ventilating, explaining, normalizing, reframing, validating. Content in itself is mental and abstract. The goal is congruence of mental and emotional aspects.

Publicity

1. Dated flyers can be used for specific beginning dates.

2. If group cycles are sequential, one following another, a "generic" flyer (without dates) may best suit your needs. It may be sent out at intervals with a request to call you for specific dates.

3. Send to:
    your own bereaved or other clientele
    public places, with a request to post (e.g. libraries, hospitals, mental & physical health agencies, etc.)

Price

$5-10/session or a lump sum up front
"Group Donations" sheet: (Sample follows)
        attached to a manila envelope, passed around each session for $ per session and
        appropriate date box checked by participant

Definition of Membership

Loss via death
   (AIDS-related losses may best be separated from "mixed" losses)
   Mixture of relationships is OK (e.g spouse, partner, sibling, friend, etc.; death is the common thread).
   Group is best closed after the 2nd session for optimal bonding

Group Number

   Maximum of 10, minimum of 5, 8 ideal.

Screening

   Screening is done in initiating phone call. Address is obtained at this time and followed
   by a letter from facilitator and "Commitment Sheet," mailed to each potential participant
   prior to group starting date. Return of the "Commitment Sheet" confirms the person's place in
   the group. (Sample follows)

Format

   8-week cycle, once a week, 2 hours/session
   A "reunion," follow-up session 1 month following the last group session
   e.g. "potluck" at a group member's house, in a restaurant, a picnic in the park, etc.

Structured:
   Each session has a particular focus on an aspect of the grief process. The (1) information & hand-
   outs, (2) group participation (check-in & sharing) and (3) an experiential exercise all reflect the focus
   of the session.

Evaluations

Distributed at the last session with stamped/addressed envelope for return to facilitator
(vs. completion before leaving session). For two reasons:

1.   An exercise for focus and closure for participants.

2.   More thought-out than an evaluation done hurriedly at the end of the session, thus
better quality feed-back

These evaluations are helpful for the facilitator to discover what works and what doesn't.
If, for example, the same comment is made on several evaluations, it might be time to
make some changes accordingly, to better meet the participants' needs.

Participants are obviously not finished their grief process in eight weeks, but are beginning
to discover glimpses of how to get "from here to there." They begin to have some idea of
a "mental map" through the territory of grief and have begun again to take hold of their
lives.

GROUP
PARTICIPATION
AGREEMENT

Name of Group: _____

Facilitator: _____

Group meets from _____to_____

I AGREE TO ...

- attend all meetings of the group.
- notify the facilitator (by leaving a message at _____ if I may be late or unable to attend a meeting.
- be on time for each group.
- stay for the full time of the group
- give my attention to others when they are speaking.
- respect the beliefs, opinions, and values of other participants.
- share my experiences, instead of generalizing or telling others what they should do.
- share my opinions and feelings about the group with the facilitator and participants, not with others outside the group.
- respect the privacy of other participants by not talking with others outside the group about what they said in group.

MY COMMITMENT TO_____IS:_____a tax-deductible donation of

_____ $80 or more for each 8-week group (attached)

_____ $10 or more paid each group session

_____ other amount (specify) $_____

_____to assist by volunteering (call to arrange)

_____I need a full/partial scholarship (call to arrange)

_____ Date:_____

Signature

_____ Home:(   )_____

Address

_____ Work:(   )_____

City/St/Zip

GROUP DONATIONS

_____
Group

Facilitator:_____

From:_____To:_____

Name Session No.	1	2	3	4	5	6	7	8

THANK YOU FOR HELPING SUPPORT_____!

We rely on donations to maintain the house and our program; we do not receive any
government funds.

Suggested donation is $80 for 8-week group. However no one is
to be denied service for financial reasons, Through our fundraising efforts, full and partial
scholarships are available. Call (   )_____.

GRIEF SUPPORT GROUP
FEEDBACK/EVALUATION

1. What were the most important things you learned from these sessions?

2. What did you like best about the sessions?

3. What is your experience of the facilitator's
    a) Effectiveness of presentations?
    b) Leading exercises?
    c) Ability to answer questions?

4. What did you like least about the sessions?

5. If you were to improve 3 things about this support group, what would they be, and how would you improve them?

6. Please comment on your experience of this group's format:
    a) Closed after second session?

    b) Do you feel more comfortable when everyone wears first-name tags for first three sessions?

    c) Do you like to exchange names & phone numbers?

    d) Information
        ___Enough   ___Too much   ___Not enough

    e) Sharing time
        ___Enough   ___Too much   ___Not enough

7. Further questions and/or comments about the group?

Thank you for your feedback!

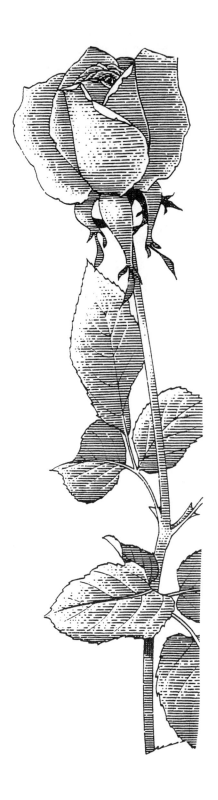

SESSION ONE

THE GRIEF PROCESS

Session 1: The Grief Process
What is Grief? Descriptions of the Grief Process
How does it affect us?

Name tags (for first 3 sessions)
Paper binders for hand-outs (to be used to store future hand-outs)
    To include:
      First week's hand-outs (as follow)
      Your card, or at least the phone number where you can be reached during the week
      Any "welcome," orientation or information statements

1. Welcome and Overview
    "Housekeeping"/Money arrangements/Purpose/Goals/Ground Rules

2. Introductions by participants:
    Say your own name
    Give the name of the person who died (or the nature of the significant loss)
    How long ago? Age? Cause of death?
    Why are you here? What do you hope to get from the group?

3. The bottom has dropped out of your world. Its structure has collapsed. As the result of having loved and lost, you will never be quite the same again. As you pull together the shattered pieces of your life, your identity will be in a revised, different configuration. Chances are, you feel:

helpless	angry	afraid/anxious	ill-equipped
depressed	inadequate	drifting/unstable	confused

4. Grief is originally an unlearned feeling process. It is a normal and natural response to loss.
    Factors which affect the grieving process; its intensity and time-frame:
    * past experiences
    * the degree to which the loss affects your daily life
    * your personality
    * support from external sources

5. Ways of describing the grief process: (hand-outs)
    * Prose, "how to," tasks, tables of stages, expectations
    * Symbols
    * Music/song
    * Dance
    * Art
    * Poetry (read 2-3 short examples)

6. We are ill-prepared to deal with loss:
    a. As children we are taught to <u>acquire</u> (for "success," to be "complete & whole")

    both: {   material "things" and

                      abstract (e.g. parents' approval, good grades, knowledge)

    b. Thus, losing something feels wrong, unnatural, broken

<u>Examples:</u>

"Don't feel bad, on Saturday we will get you a new bike/dog/friend
teaches: 1) bury, reject, suppress your feelings
          2) your loss can be replaced

"Don't disturb your mother. She'll be OK in a little while."
teaches: 3) grieve alone, let others grieve alone
          4) time will "fix" it

"You're grieving, but you'll get over it."
teaches: 5) just give it time
          6) you don't have to "do" anything (no self-responsibility)

Other messages you may have heard:
          7) Regret the past ("should" have been DIFFERENT, BETTER, MORE)
          8) Don't trust
          9) Be seen and not heard
          10) Protect yourself
          11) Don't get involved, they'll only leave you anyway
          12) Get all you can before it's taken away from you
          13) Don't expect anything

7. Exercise: Drawings (Allow 45-60 minutes for drawing and sharing)
    a. Each participant receives a 15" x 20" drawing paper
    b. Assorted crayons, pastels available for selection
    c. Lead group in short relaxation exercise to get in touch with inner world of feeling:

3

Relaxation Exercise:

Close your eyes and get as comfortable as you can in your chair. Take a deep, slow breath in and s-l-o-w-l-y let it out through your mouth. Imagine you are breathing out any tension in your body. . . Take another deep breath in and as you s-l-o-w-l-y breathe it out, allow your head to rest comfortably on your neck, let your shoulders drop. Let you body settle into the chair. . . Another deep breath in and allow the slow exhale to relax your arms and legs, let them feel warm and heavy, your feet heavy on the floor. Take this time to withdraw into yourself, a place where it is safe, where there is no need for interaction with others. . . Imagine yourself in a closed inner world. . . You will probably notice that your mind has relatively stilled. . . Thoughts are not chasing each other as they usually do..

Now allow your attention to focus on how you feel. . . How would you describe the feeling? Does it have a name?... A color?... A shape?... A texture?... See if it could be represented by an image or a picture... Perhaps it could be described with a sound or a phrase from a song; not everyone sees images... As you are ready, allow yourself to return to the room and draw the symbol or image or picture that came to you.

If a picture or image doesn't come to you, start with the color. Pick up a crayon of that color and just see what happens when you put it to the paper.

d. Have participants put names on their drawings
e. Each participant talks about his/her drawing to the group
  (For anyone who could/would not draw, perhaps the clean sheet represents "emptiness" or you might ask, "If you couldn't draw it, tell us what you would have drawn if you were able.")
f. Collect the drawings (to be returned at the 8th session when the exercise is repeated and the two drawings are compared.)

8. Closure

(Reach out and join hands while everyone remains seated)

Notice the difference in your own feelings and the feeling of the group now, compared to the feeling when you first came in. We came in as strangers to each other and already there is a difference as we have shared our common bond of loss. This indeed can be a healing circle. Take a minute to appreciate the courage it took to come here and to share these very tender feelings with strangers. Imagine yourself sending warmth, caring and compassion through your right arm to the person holding your right hand... And now notice yourself receiving the warmth, caring and compassion up your left arm and into your heart from the person on your left. Tune into that feeling of receiving comfort as you go through the week.

✳✳✳✳✳

It is important in this first session that participants be given plenty of time to tell their stories and reveal their feelings. It is via the shared feelings that the group bonds.

Make sure each participant gets the opportunity to talk, but no one should feel pressured to speak it she/he would rather not. Anyone should be allowed to "pass" at any time or be skipped and returned to later. In almost every group there is at least one person, at the other extreme, who, given free rein, will take more than his/her share of time. Other group members lose interest, so gently but firmly stop the talker and start the next person.

Grief support Group

Purpose:

To provide a safe and supportive environment for the healing journey of grief. To share and begin to work through grief about a significant loss.

Goals:

1. A combination of information, personal sharing and experiential exercises to balance thinking/ feeling needs.
2. Participants will:
   - learn to give and receive support
   - learn new ways to cope with and respond to grief.
   - feel less isolated/alone with the experience.
   - receive permission to trust, express and honor feelings.
   - Learn what normal grief may look and feel like.

Ground Rules:

1. Commitment
2. Confidentiality
3. Any emotional expression OK, as long as it does not disrupt the group
4. One person speaking at a time; talking for each person limited by time in relation to number in the group. Anyone can "pass".
5. *Presence* as other members speak - attention, listening
6. Group conflict/ disturbance to be addressed at the time, in the group
7. Start and end on time!

THE WORK OF MOURNING

It is agreed by psychologists who write on the grief process, that each person must go through the important "work of mourning." This work can be quickly described, but not quickly or easily accomplished. The work of mourning requires the weakening and final breaking of every emotional tie which chains you to the past, and every expectation for the future which binds you to the person you have lost.

Only by doing this can you ever be emotionally free to build a new life for yourself. Breaking these ties can be so painful it is amazing that each person can endure the hurt it requires. It is also amazing that this pain in the lives of those who grieve is so disparaged by others. No matter how reluctantly grief work is experienced, it must be done. The pain cannot be avoided; it must be gone through.

As you are faced with days, weeks, months of a new life, you will begin to break the emotional ties that bind you in three ways: (1) by the decrease in private remembering that you now experience constantly - by the welcome but painful reminders that pour into your mind every day; (2) by talking, by sharing your feelings and your thoughts with people who will listen empathetically - the listening that is the greatest gift friends can offer; and (3) less frequently, by writing. The thinking, the talking, the writing need to go on freely as long as you require them.

Adapted from "The Work of Mourning,"

THE SYMPTOMS OF GRIEF

When we think of grief, we often think only of death, but other losses bring on almost identical reactions. People going through a divorce experience grief; so do people who have lost good health. Grief is also common to the aging person. A man in his mid-60's facing mandatory retirement may show grief-like responses. Parents may experience grief as their children grow up and leave home.

Ten symptoms of grief are commonly seen by doctors, counselors, religious and others who deal with emotional problems. Everyone experiences some or all of these symptoms whenever he/she loses something or someone very important. In other words, what we are really talking about is "good grief," the normal response to loss, the process of grieving. Recognizing and dealing with this healthy kind of grief can help a person move through response to a significant loss.

SHOCK

We become temporarily anesthetized, numb against the reality of the event. This state of shock is protective to our emotional well-being. We do not have to comprehend the magnitude of the loss all at once.

EMOTIONAL RELEASE

This stage occurs when the dreadful loss begins to be realized. People sometimes need to be encouraged to express their feelings and to recognize that emotional release is normal and appropriate. Many of us have learned to deny these unpleasant feelings. We have been taught to admire people who "cope, are brave, get back to normal quickly."

DEPRESSION, LONELINESS, SENSE OF ISOLATION

We experience the depths of despair, begin to withdraw and limit our social interaction, and believe there is no hope for the future. We may feel depressed, isolated and alone.

PHYSICAL SYMPTOMS OF DISTRESS

One study show that 80% of people seeking medical treatment have suffered a loss during the preceding six months. Problems with sleep or with over - or under - eating are common. It is not unusual for survivors to experience symptoms similar to those of their dead loved one. Competent and compassionate medical help and an understanding of the grief process are often both necessary and helpful.

PANIC

Anxiety sets in when we are unable to concentrate on anything except our loss. We find it difficult to focus on anything else. Dreams or "hallucinations" are often so distressing we fear losing our mind. It is helpful to know that these responses are normal, natural, to be expected and, in other cultures, are actually anticipated.

GUILT, REGRETS

Guilt and/or regrets about everything related to the loss are also normal responses. As such, they need to be expressed and worked through. It may be helpful to draw up a balance sheet: regrets in one column, balanced by a second column acknowledging all the helpful, supportive contributions.

ANGER AND RESENTMENT

When we have someone or something precious taken away from us, angry resentment is a normal response. Anger is also a sign that depression is lifting. It is a very powerful emotion and, if expressed in a supportive environment, can be energizing.

RESISTANCE TO RETURN TO USUAL ACTIVITIES

Although, at this time, grieving feels more familiar and comfortable, it is still painful for us to contemplate facing the world again, alone. We need to be encouraged and compassionately helped to return to normal daily activities.

A GLIMPSE OF HOPE

Little by little, emotional balance begins to return, with support and encouragement. It is impossible to predict when this stage will occur, due to the range of individual differences.

ACKNOWLEDGMENT OF REALITY

We do not become our "old selves" again. We are never our "old selves" after a major grief experience. We are intrinsically different from before. But we realize that it IS possible to go on with our lives... to live and laugh and love again.

Adapted from Good Grief by Granger Westberg, Philadelphia: Fortress Press, 1976

GRIEF: A <u>Response</u> to Loss or Separation

	Lindemann	Engel	Kubler-Ross	Bowlby
Shock: "Closing off" Period	Somatic Distress Preoccupation of image Guilt Feelings Hostility Loss of Patterns of Conduct	Shock/Disbelief	Denial Anger	Protest
Suffering: "Opening up" Period Disorganization, Guilt, Volatile Emotions, Disengagement Loss, loneliness		Developing Awareness	Anger Bargaining Depression	Despair Detachment
Renewal: Catharsis & Healing Relief / re-establishment		Restitution	_____ Acceptance	Personality Reorganization

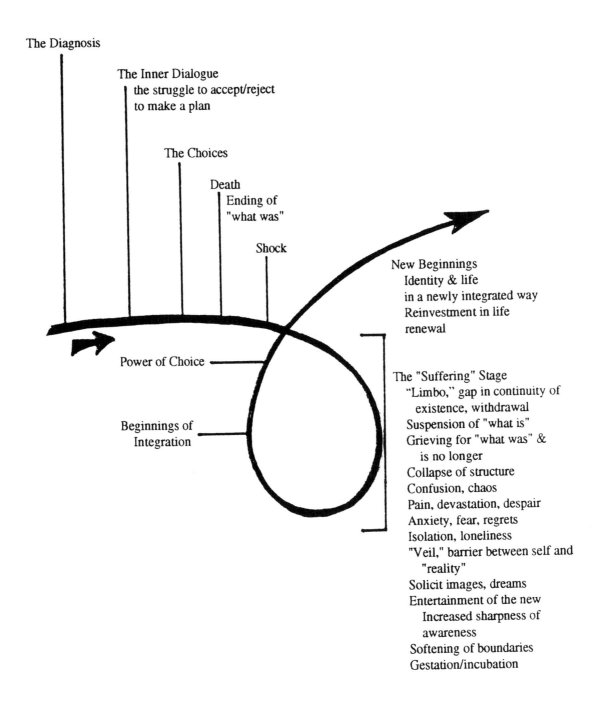

The Diagnosis

The Inner Dialogue
the struggle to accept/reject
to make a plan

The Choices

Death
Ending of
"what was"

Shock

New Beginnings
Identity & life
in a newly integrated way
Reinvestment in life
renewal

Power of Choice

Beginnings of
Integration

The "Suffering" Stage
"Limbo," gap in continuity of
existence, withdrawal
Suspension of "what is"
Grieving for "what was" &
is no longer
Collapse of structure
Confusion, chaos
Pain, devastation, despair
Anxiety, fear, regrets
Isolation, loneliness
"Veil," barrier between self and
"reality"
Solicit images, dreams
Entertainment of the new
Increased sharpness of
awareness
Softening of boundaries
Gestation/incubation

**The Transition Loop
for the Grief Process**

©: Anne C. Grant, PhD

THE GRIEVING PROCESS

NORMAL GRIEF PROCESS

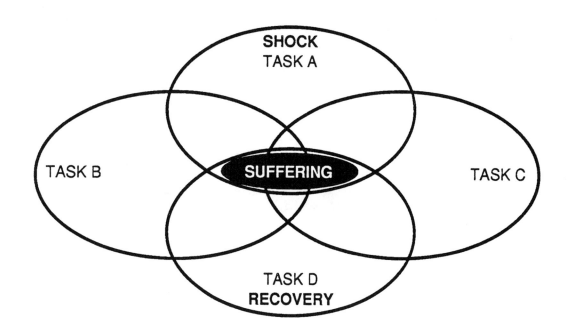

Task of Grief

A. Accept the realty of the loss

B. Identify and express feelings -- experience the pain of grief

C. Adjust to environment in which deceased is missing

D. Withdraw emotional energy from the deceased and reinvest in other outlets.

Grief Counseling and Grief Therapy by William Worden, Reprinted with permission Springer Publishing, Inc.

GRIEF WHEEL

Ability to reconnect and invest energy in relationships and activities

RECOVERY

LOSS

SHOCK

* Numbness, outbursts, denial, weight loss, blunting

PROTEST

* Anger, yearning, crying, increased affect, Irritibality.
* Loss of appetite or increased eating.
* Preoccupation with thoughts of the deceased.
* Searching, avoiding, nausea, guilt, self-criticism.
* Physical symptoms, sleep disturbance, weakness, exhaustion, sighing, shortness of breath.
* Increased use of alcohol or drugs, leading towards depression

REORGANIZATION

* Trying new patterns of behavior
* Finding meaning in death & life.
* New intrest skills.
* New or renewed socialization

DISORGANIZATION

* Confusion, Depression, Withdrawal, Loneliness
* Aimlessness, Restlessness, Apathy
* Sense of presence, feeling of unreality.
* Decreased socialization, loss of intrest.

13

Grieving: A Model

page 160-161

page 133

page 111

page 15

A holistic framework for the phases of grief

Look at this symbol as though the loss was a pebble dropped into a still pool, the waves/phases radiating out from the loss with decreasing intensity.

"Phase" implies a transient quality - a few moments or much longer.

There is no structural order; phases are repeated or recycled, perhaps occurring several times during the course of grieving

Adapted from *Stress, Loss and Grief* by John Schnaider, Aspen Publishers, Inc.

INITIAL AWARENESS

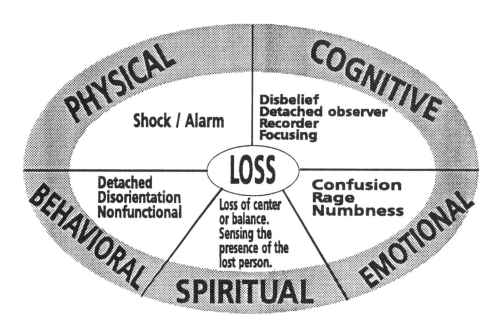

The reality of the loss has reached conscious awareness. It is usually experienced as a shock to the system, both physically and mentally, representing an intrusion of a new reality. There is often a disruption of the capacity to function.

It is like the "alarm" stage of stress when a person mobilizes for either fight or flight. For this loss, neither is appropriate or effective, which increases the stress.

PHASE I

D
E
A
T
H

STUNNED
DISBELIEF

SHOCK
ANGER
(EVEN
HYSTERIA)
GUILT

EMPTINESS

RESTLESSNESS

DEPRESSION

PHASE II

**Facing The Reality,
Going Through The
Work Of Morning.**

PHASE III

**The Pain lessens.
This experience grows.
Healing begins.
You remember with
less pain.**

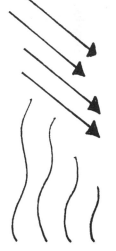

A

ACCEPTANCE

DIMINISHING
GRIEF

**What Is Difficult
At The Beginning
Becomes Easy At The End.
And Bitter
Turns Into Sweet
Chinese Proverb
Translation Lin Yutang**

16

THE HANDS OF GRIEF

Empty Hands

Emptiness, loneliness, being incomplete

Holding our head in our hands

Lamenting, releasing our thoughts & feelings, sharing our tears
Death & loss cause hurt
We need to grieve from the very depths of our heart/soul/person

Clenched hands

Image of protest, what has happened is not fair, "Why me?"
Sometimes we need to give ourself permission to protest against God

Outstretched & Joined Hands

Support systems, resource persons, a fellowship of support network to which we belong

Raised & Uplifted Hands

Pieces to be picked up, new dreams to be created, new hopes to be fulfilled, new paths to be traveled

There will be new life even though I will always bear the marks of my grief.

Source Unknown

<u>Steven</u>

he surrounded me with arms
when his tall chest pressed me into our future
and he touched my face with breath and life;
he filled my body with all the parts of him,
smiled sensuous sound into my ears with his tongue;
my body believed his body
my mind accepted his measured voice
my lips returned wet air trapped in his moustache
my ears had faith
my back believed the exquisite curve in his neck was
      bending toward me
and I smelled the fire under his mantel; I was
      surrounded by his wood;
I inhaled his smoke
and I moved to him, under his sky
      into his damp, harsh wind;
      into his house surrounded by fog
and I became the hills he climbed with his striving legs
and I was the sweet melon he ate when he came in;
      and we drank each other
      and it was the way it would be forever

now, I miss him, sometimes
I miss his body when I remember the sunny days
I miss being told what I wanted to hear
I miss him when I forget the newspaper stuffed in the
      chimney of the fireplace we never used
I miss feeling his warm face nuzzled next to me in the
      morning when fog obliterated the rest of the city
and I miss him when I forget that he's still up there,
sometimes, I think of him, lovingly,
now that I've come back to a sunny neighborhood with
      easy transportation
I miss him, sometimes, in my new life, alone

ONE DAY AT A TIME

Just for today I will try to live through this day only. I will not think about the future. I know I can get through just one day.

Just for today if I feel angry I will find a safe way to express it. I may scream and beat a pillow, but I will not hurt anyone.

Just for today I will remember the good things and let go of blame and regret because no one can change the past.

Just for today I will have a plan to fill the time. I will avoid idle hours which can lead to depression and despair.

Just for today I will set aside some time to relax and I will plan a short-term goal to work toward.

Just for today I will have hope that life will get better because love never dies and love can sustain us through the most painful tragedies.

Just for today I will be unafraid. Especially I will not be afraid to enjoy what is beautiful because my life must go on.

Just for today I will have faith that even though life is not always fair, it is still worth living. In time, with faith and the grace of God, I will find new meaning in my life.

Anonymous
Source Unknown

Since Kathy Died

By Dr. Robert Kirsch

EDITOR'S NOTE: *The death of Dr. Kirsch's wife, Kathy, occurred just one day after the birth of their fourth child. That child is now nine years old.*

A roller-coaster, merry go-round existence.
Awash upon a sea of conflicting emotions.
Tossed about and buffeted by fate.
One moment up, the next down,
As patches of memory steal across each day.

Pressurized and smothered by solicitous well-wishing.
Queries hurled from every side which I cannot rejoin.
Matters once resolved.
Tucked away in comfortable mental niches,
Now return unanswered and unanswerable.

Doubt, bitterness, frustration, emptiness, loneliness
All jumbled into one.
A dozen years of happy marriage terminated.
Eligible again for the mating game,
I am uncertain how to play.

Adolescence recurs with a vengeance.
Fantasy tantalizes and distorts reality.
Perception poisoned by longing for closeness and intimacy
Lost but never forgotten.

Together in love we charted our life,
Separated by death, love lives on.

Though my lover is dead,
We meet in my dreams,
Dreams so real they stir me from sleep,
Rekindling that awful ache,
As I sit trembling on the edge of my empty bed.

Daily, I struggle to recreate a meaningful life,
Prodded by recognition of my children's anxieties and needs,
That my lot is not solitary.

Confronted by ever-nagging uncertainty.
Knowing only vaguely whence I have come
Or where I am bound.

Reprinted with permission Bereavement Magazine/June 1990

C.S. Lewis
1898-1963

Lewis Originally published this private journal under the pseudonym N. W. Clerk, a pun on Old English for "I know not what scholar."

---

from *A Grief Observed*

No one ever told me that grief felt so like fear. I am not afraid, but the sensation is like being afraid. The same fluttering in the stomach, the same restlessness, the yawning. I keep on swallowing.

At other times it feels like being mildly drunk, or concussed. There is a sort of invisible blanket between the world and me. I find it hard to take it in. It is so uninteresting. Yet I want the others to be about me. I dread the moments when the house is empty. If only they would talk to one another and not to me.

There are moments, most unexpectedly, when something inside me tries to assure me that I don't really mind so much, not so very much, after all. Love is not the whole of a man's life. I was happy before I ever met H. I've plenty of what are called "resources." People get over these things. Come, I shan't do so badly. One is ashamed to listen to this voice but it seems for a little to be making out a good case. Then comes a sudden jab of red-hot memory and all this "commonsense" vanishes like an ant in the mouth of a furnace....

And no one ever told me about the laziness of grief. Except at my job - where the machine seems to run much as usual - I loathe the slightest effort. Not only writing but even reading a letter is too much. Even shaving. What does it matter now whether my cheek is rough or smooth? They say an unhappy man wants distractions - something to take him out of himself. Only as a dog-tired man wants an extra blanket on a cold night; he'd rather lie there shivering than get up and find one. It's easy to see why the lonely become untidy; finally dirty and disgusting....

I cannot talk to the children about her. The moment I try, there appears on their faces neither grief, nor love, nor fear, nor pity, but the most fatal of all non-conductors, embarrassment. They look as if I were committing an indecency. They are longing for me to stop. I felt just the same after my own mother's death when my father mentioned her. I can't blame them. It's the way boys are....

It isn't only the boys either. An odd by-product of my loss is that I'm aware of being an embarrassment to everyone I meet. At work, at the club, in the street, I see people, as they approach me, trying to make up their minds whether they'll "say something about it" or not. I hate it if they do, and if they don't. Some funk it altogether. R. has been avoiding me for a week. I like best the well brought-up young men, almost boys, who walk up to me as if I were a dentist, turn very red, get it over, and then edge away to the bar as quickly as they decently can. Perhaps the bereaved ought to be isolated in special settlements like lepers....

...There is one place where her absence comes locally home to me, and it is a place I can't avoid. I mean my own body. It had such a different importance while it was the body of H.'s lover. Now it's like an empty house. But don't let me deceive myself. This body would become important to me again, and pretty quickly, if I thought there was anything wrong with it....

It is hard to have patience with people who say "There is no death" or "Death doesn't matter." There is death. And whatever is matters. And whatever happens has consequences, and it and they are irrevocable and irreversible. You might as well say that birth doesn't matter. I look up at the night sky. Is anything more certain that in all those vast times and spaces, if I were allowed to search them, I should nowhere find her face, her voice, her touch? She died. She is dead? Is the word so difficult to learn?...

Talk to me about the truth of religion and I'll listen gladly. Talk to me about the duty of religion and I'll listen submissively. But don't come talking to me about the consolations of religion or I shall suspect that you don't understand.

...Aren't all these notes the senseless writings of a man who won't accept the fact that there is nothing we can do with suffering except to suffer it? Who still thinks there is some device (if only he could find it) which will make pain not to be pain. It doesn't really matter whether you grip the arms of the dentist's chair or let your hands lie in your lap. The drill drills on....

It's not true that I'm always thinking of H. Work and conversation make that impossible. But the times when I'm not are perhaps my worst. For then, though I have forgotten the reason, there is spread over everything a vague sense of wrongness, of something amiss. Like in those dreams where nothing terrible occurs - nothing that would sound even remarkable if you told it at breakfast-time - but the atmosphere, the taste of the whole thing is deadly. So with this. I see the rowan berries reddening and don't know for a moment why they, of all things, should be depressing. I hear a clock strike and some quality it always had before has gone out of the sound. What's wrong with the world to make it so flat, shabby, worn-out looking? Then I remember.

What sort of lover am I to think so much about my affliction and so much less about hers? Even the insane call, "Come back," is all for my own sake. I never even raised the question whether such a return, if it were possible, would be good for her. I want her back as an ingredient in the restoration of my past. Could I have wished her anything worse? Having got once through death, to come back and then, at some later date, have all her dying to do over again? They call Stephen the first martyr. Hadn't Lazarus the rawer deal?...

Something quite unexpected has happened. It came this morning early. For various reasons, not in themselves all mysterious, my heart was lighter than it had been for many weeks. For one thing, I suppose I am recovering physically from a good deal of mere exhaustion. And I'd had a very tiring but very healthy twelve hours the day before, and a sounder night's sleep; and after ten days of low-hung grey skies and motionless warm dampness, the sun was shining and there was a light breeze. And suddenly at the very moment when, so far, I mourned H. least, I remembered her best. Indeed it was something (almost) better than memory; an instantaneous, unanswerable impression. To say it was like a meeting would be going too far. Yet there was that in it which tempts one to use those words. It was as if the lifting of sorrow removed a barrier.

Why has no one told me these things? How easily I might have misjudged another man in the same situation? I might have said, "he's got over it. He's forgotten his wife," when the truth was, "He remembers her better *because* he has partly got over it."

...There's no denying that in some sense I "feel better," and with that comes at once a sort of shame, and a feeling that one is under a sort of obligation to cherish and foment and prolong one's unhappiness. I've read about that in books, but I never dreamed I should feel it myself. I am sure. H. wouldn't approve of it. She'd tell me not to be a fool....

This is the fourth - and the last - empty MS. book I can find in the house; at least nearly empty, for there are some pages of very ancient arithmetic at the end by J. I resolve to let this limit my jottings. I *will not* start buying books for this purpose. In so far as this record was a defence against total collapse, a safety-valve, it has done some good. The other end I had in view turns out to have been based on a misunderstanding. I thought I could describe a *state*; make a map of sorrow. Sorrow, however, turns out to be not a state but a process. It needs not a map but a history, and if I don't stop writing that history at some quite arbitrary point, there's no reason why I should ever stop. There is something new to be chronicled every day. Grief is like a long valley, a winding valley where any bend may reveal a totally new landscape. As I've already noted, not every bend does. Sometimes the surprise is the opposite one; you are presented with exactly the same sort of country you thought you had left behind miles ago. That is when you wonder whether the valley isn't a circular trench. But it isn't. There are partial recurrences, but the sequence doesn't repeat.

Here, for instance, is a new phase, a new loss. I do all the walking I can, for I'd be a fool to go to bed not tired. Today I have been revisiting old haunts, taking in one of the long rambles that made me happy in my bachelor days. And this time the face of nature was not emptied of its beauty and the world didn't look (as I complained some days ago) like a mean street. On the contrary, every horizon, every stile or clump of trees, summoned me into a past kind of happiness, my pre-H. happiness. But the invitation seemed to me horrible. The happiness into which it invited me was insipid. I find that I don't want to go back again and be happy in *that* way. It frightens me to think that a mere going back should even be possible. For this fate would seem to me the worst of all; to reach a state in which my years of love and marriage should appear in retrospect a charming episode - like a holiday - that had briefly interrupted my interminable life and returned me to normal, unchanged. And then it would come to seem unreal - something so foreign to the usual texture of my history that I could almost believe it had happened to someone else. Thus H. would die to me a second time; a worse bereavement than the first. Anything but that....

It is often thought that the dead see us. And we assume, whether reasonably or not, that if they see us at all they see us more clearly than before. Does H. now see exactly how much froth or tinsel there was in what she called, and I call, my love? So be it. Look your hardest, dear. I wouldn't hide it if I could. We didn't idealize each other. We tried to keep no secrets. You knew most of the rotten places in me already. If you now see anything worse, I can take it. So can you. Rebuke, explain, mock, forgive. For this is one of the miracles of love; it gives - to both, but perhaps especially to the woman - a power of seeing through its own enchantments and yet not being disenchanted....

I said, several notebooks ago, that even if I got what seemed like a assurance of H.'s presence, I wouldn't believe it. Easier said than done. Even now, though, I won't treat anything of that sort as evidence. It's the *quality* of last night's experience - not what it proves but what it was - that makes it worth putting down. It was quite incredibl unemotional. Just the impression of her *mind* momentarily facing my own. Mind, not "soul" as we tend to think of soul. Certainly the reverse of what we call "soulful." Not at all like a rapturous re-union of lovers. Much more like getting a telephone call or a wire from her about some practical arrangement. Not that there was any "message" - just intelligence and attention. No sense of joy or sorrow. No love even, in our ordinary sense. No un-love. I had never in any mood imagined the dead as being so - well, so business-like. Yet there was an extreme and cheerful intimacy. An intimacy that had not passed through the senses or the emotions at all.

Exerpt from <u>In The Midst of Winter</u> by Mary Jane Moffat, Ed., Harper & Collins, Reprinted with permission

NORMAL GRIEF EXPERIENCES

Physical Sensations

1. Stomach: hollowness, "butterflies," hunger, nausea, loss of appetite
2. Chest, throat: pain, tightness, breathlessness
3. Dry mouth, increased perspiration
4. Shakiness
5. Headaches
6. Lack of energy; overall weakness
7. Overly sensitive to noise
8. Sense of depersonalization: "Nothing seems real"
9. Same physical symptoms as deceased's illness

Thoughts

1. Disbelief: "Oh, no!" "It's not happening to me"
2. Confusion, forgetfulness
3. Preoccupation or obsessive thinking about the deceased
4. Finality: "Things will bever be the same," "You can't go back"
5. Anger: "it's not fair," "Why did it happen?"
6. "If only..." "I wish..."
7. Forging ahead: "I have to make some decisions," "I have to get through it"
8. Paranormal experiences: sense of presence, visual, auditory, tactile, olfactory, dreams
9. Dread: fear of own or other's death
10. Suicide: "Life has no meaning"

Behaviors

1. Sleeping and appetite disturbances
2. Crying, sighing
3. Absent-minded behavior
4. Searching behavior; expecting the deceased
5. Social withdrawal
6. Marked increase or decrease in activity; restlessness
7. Increase in illness/accidents
8. Change in work performance: late, leaving early or working late, not meeting deadlines, shutting office door, eating alone
9. Yelling
10. Increased alcohol/drug/nicotine intake
11. Sloppy dressing; poor personal hygeine
12. Activity regarding the deceased: searching & calling out, visiting places or treasuring objects as reminders of the deceased, talking to deceased's picture or ashes

Feelings

1. Sadness
2. Anger, frustration, irritation, misdirected hostility
3. Depression
4. Guilt
5. Victimized, helpless, out of control, futility
6. Not being valued
7. Loneliness
8. Shock, numbness
9. Yearning
10. Fear
11. Relief
12. Peace, resolution

SESSION TWO

ENHANCING TRUST IN/CARE OF SELF

Session 2: Enhancing Trust in/Care of Self

Is it OK to focus attention on me?
What about friends' advice to be strong/brave/get on with life?

1. Overview of the session (set the "stage" for check-in-)
   When you are grieving, *you* are the focus. Grieving is about *your* emotional
   experience of loss. While we are not *blaming* the lost person for leaving (it wasn't
   necessarily his choice); while we can be glad he is no longer suffering, this does not
   change *your* empty feeling of being abandoned, of having to pick up the pieces of your
   shattered life and muddle on alone. Your needs are unique. No matter how much a
   scenario looks the same, for each of you there is a unique grief process because *you*
   are each different. There is no one *right way* to grieve. Each of you also has a unique
   sequence and time frame.

   We have to assume that friends mean well. They are often very free with advice, but
   what works for them may not at all work for you. Often the advice is from their
   minds, while grieving is *about* feelings. When you are in a feeling mode and they are
   in a mental mode, there is no way of connection and you are left feeling unperceived
   and unsatisfied by the interaction.

   Each of us has an inner sense of our own needs and I encourage you to access and
   honor those unique needs. Listen to your friends, do an inner check and use the
   advice that feels right, reject that which does not apply or doesn't fit your way of
   process.

2. Introductions/Check In
   Give your name.
   Give the name of the person you are mourning.
   Tell us your response or experience of friends' advice in relationship to your own
   needs. Or just tell us how your week went.

3. Brainstorming
   - What kinds of things do people say to you that feel helpful? That are unhelpful?
   - Is there something you would like to hear and don't?
   - When you hear helpful things, how does it make you feel inside?
   - When you hear unhelpful things?
   - Stay in touch with your own inner needs; screen advice selectively according to
     what feels appropriate for those needs.

4. Four ways to deal with suffering (Following, p.30)

5. Others are ill-prepared to help us deal with loss (Following, p.31)

6. Exercise: (To clarify feelings and experience and validate your needs)
   Heart, mind, spirit & body: all need nurture/replenishment
A. Given that you would probably all choose to have your loved person back, in the reality of your loss:
   *• Write a statement starting with the words "I need..."
      e.g.   to feel free to rest, do nothing
              to share my feelings
              to let it be OK to be angry
   • With that statement in mind, what is the nicest and kindest experience you could give yourself to honor that need?
   • Is there any part of yourself that denies you deserve this experience?
B. <u>Or</u> Exploration of the wounds of Grief (Following, p.32)

7. Closure
   Join hands, while remaining seated.
   Notice how differently each of us reacts to a statement meant to be comforting.
   Imagine yourself putting into the center of the circle a statement, or a feeling, or an action you have found to be comforting and imagine their blending there...
   Imagine yourself now basking in that comfort, just immerse yourself in this blended loving and compassionate feeling...During the coming week, if you need it, put yourself back in this space...and have a good week.

*A. Distribute pencils and pads of paper.
   Given that you would......

Four Ways To Deal With Suffering

1. Suppression
   - The attempt to forget it, to smile even if it hurts; the smile is a grimace--we can't ignore what is there

2. Living the pain, but living it only halfway
   - A draining identification with suffering begins and it may color every other aspect of our life.
   - Then the pain sticks with us--as too big a bite will stick in the throat, refusing to go down or come up. "I can't swallow that."

3. Living our grief fully, consciously & intensely--for the purpose of becoming free from it.
   - Having given it full expression, we can shatter its paralyzing grip and begin to detach from it.
   - It still exists, but it is no longer so deeply infused with our being, so closely identified with our life.
   - When it is no longer darkly shut within, we make a space between suffering & ourselves.

4. Transform it:
   Into useful & beautiful actions, artistic & humanistic endeavors.

Source Unknown

Others Are Ill-Prepared To Help Us Deal With Loss

- They don't know what to say
    (no personal experience or knowledge of others)
    They're afraid of our feelings
    Get a hold of yourself (Get a grip)
    You can't fall apart
    Keep a stiff upper lip
    Pull yourself up by the bootstraps
    Be strong for the children

- They try to change the subject
    let's deal with our feelings by changing the subject

- They intellectualize (when grieving is *about* feelings)
    We understand how you feel
    Be thankful you have another son
    The living must go on
    All things must pass
    She led a full life
    You'll find someone else

- They think keeping "busy" helps

- They don't want to talk about death
    She passed away
    He's gone to his eternal rest
    Dad's gone
    He expired
    We've lost Mother

- They want us to keep our faith
    You shouldn't be angry with God

- They want their help to be effective

Exploration of the Wound of Grief

How long is it? How wide? How deep?

What vital parts docs it touch?

Is it a clean cut? Or a jagged tear? A puncture?

Is there anything in it? Is it bleeding?

Where does it hurt? How does it hurt?

How long ago did this happen? What did you do?

Will is affect your function? Will it heal?

What scars will you have? How will they look?

What are you feeling? Are you afraid? Of what?

Source Unknown

DO WE HAVE AS MUCH SENSE AS
A GOOSE?

This fall when you see geese heading south for the winter, flying along in "V" formation, you might be interested in knowing what science has discovered about why they fly that way. It has been learned that as each bird flaps its wings, it creates an uplift for the bird immediately following, the whole flock adds at least 71 percent greater flying range than if each bird flew on its own. (People who share a common direction and sense of community can get where they are going quicker and easier because they are traveling on the thrust of one another.)

Whenever a goose falls out of formation, it suddenly feels the drag and resistance of trying to go it alone, and quickly gets back into formation to take advantage of the lifting power of the bird immediately in front. (If we have as much sense as a goose, we will stay in formation with those who are headed the same way we are going.) When the lead goose gets tired, he rotates back in the wing and another goose flies point. (It pays to take turns doing the hard jobs.) The geese honk from behind to encourage those up front to keep up the speed. (What do we say when we honk from behind?)

Finally, (now I want you to get this) when a goose gets sick or is wounded by gunshot and falls out, two geese fall out of formation and follow it down to help and protect it. They stay with the goose until it is either able to fly or until it is dead. Then they launch out on their own or with another formation, to catch up with their group. (If we have the sense of a goose, we will stand by each other like that.)

Reprinted with permission
From HARLEQUIN HAPPENINGS of Olympic Peninsula Audubon Society.
"anonymous" per Doris Smith

33

Appropriate Expectations You Can Have for Yourself in Grief

* Your grief will take longer than most people think.

* Your grief will take more energy than you would have ever imagined.

* Your grief will involve many changes and be continually developing.

* Your grief will show itself in all spheres of your life: psychological, social and physical. Response to a major loss is more global than we are prepared for.

* Your grief will depend on how you perceive the loss.

* You will grieve for many things both symbolic and tangible, not just the death alone.

* You will grieve for what you have lost already and for what you have lost for the future.

* Your grief will entail mourning not only for the actual person you lost but also for all of the hopes, dreams, and unfulfilled expectations you held for and with that person, and for the needs that will go un-met because of the death.

* Your grief will involve a wide variety of feelings and reactions, not solely those that are generally thought of as grief, such as depression and sadness.

* The loss will resurrect old issues, feelings and unresolved conflicts from the past.

* You will have some identity confusion as a result of this major loss and will probably experience reactions that may be quite different for you.

* You may have a combination of anger and depression, such as irritability, frustration, annoyance or intolerance.

* You may have a lack of self-concern.

* You may experience grief spasms, acute upsurges of grief that occur suddenly with no warning.

* You will have trouble thinking (memory, organization and intellectual processing) and making decisions.

* You may feel like you are going crazy.

* You may be obsessed with the death and preoccupied with the deceased.

* You may begin a search for meaning and may question your religion and/or philosophy of life.

* You may find yourself acting socially in ways that are different from before.

* You may find yourself having a number of physical reactions.

* Society will have unreal expectations about your mourning and may respond inappropriately to you.

* You may find there are certain dates, events and stimuli (e.g. special song, locations, etc.) that bring upsurges of grief.

* Certain experiences or events later in life may resurrect intense grief for you temporarily.

From: Grieving: How to go on Living When Someone You Love Dies Reprinted with permission Rando, Therese, Macmillan Publishing Company, 1988.

MYTHS & UNREALISTIC Expectations of Grief

All losses are the same.

It takes two months to get over your grief.

All bereaved people grieve in the same way.

Grief always declines over time in a steadily decreasing fashion.

When grief is resolved, it never comes up again.

Family members will always help grievers.

It is better to put painful things out of your mind.

You should not think about your deceased loved one at anniversaries or holidays because it will make you too sad.

Bereaved people need only to express their feelings and they will resolve their grief.

Expressing feelings that are intense is the same as losing control.

There is no reason to be angry at people who tried to do their best for your loved one.

There is no reason to be angry with your deceased loved one.

Only sick individuals have physical problems in grief.

Because you feel crazy, you are going crazy.

You should feel only sadness that your loved one has died.

Rituals and funerals are unimportant in helping us deal with life and death in contemporary America.

You will be the same after the death as before your loved one died.

You will have no relationship with your loved one after the death.

The intensity and length of your grief are testimony to you love for him/her.

There is something wrong if you do not always feel close to your friends and family, since you should be happy that they are still alive.

If someone has lost a spouse, he or she knows what it is like to lose a child.

When in doubt about what to say to a bereaved person, offer a cliché.

It is better to tell bereaved people to "Be brave" and "Keep a stiff upper lip" because then they will not have to experience as much pain.

Grief will affect you psychologically, but in no other way.

If you are a widow, you should grieve like other widows.

You will not be affected much if your parent dies when you are an adult.

It is not important for you to have social support in your grief.

Once a loved one has died it is better not to focus on him or her, but to put him or her in the past and go on with your life.

You can find ways to avoid the pain of your grief and still resolve it successfully.

How many of these statements do you believe? Each one of them is a myth. None of them is true. Yet, if you believe that they are true you will expect yourself to act and feel accordingly.

From: Grieving: How to go on Living When Someone You Love Dies, Reprinted with permission Rando, Therese, Macmillian Publishing Company, 1988.

SUGGESTIONS FOR COPING WITH GRIEF

Here are some understandings about grief and some resources to be called forth to cope with the sometimes overwhelming symptoms of loss.

UNDERSTANDINGS

Grief is a normal and natural response to loss. It is originally an unlearned feeling process. Keeping grief inside increases your pain.

Grief is a process, not a state. There are three major phases:
Shock, denial, disbelief, avoidance, numbness: a "closing off" period
> Just as the body goes into shock after a physical trauma, so does the human psyche go into shock after the impact of a major loss.

Suffering, confrontation: the "opening up" period
> The period of time when your grief is experienced most intensely, when you really begin to learn that your loved person is gone, that your life is irrevocably changed.

New beginnings, renewal, re-establishment: catharsis and healing
> A gradual decline in your grief, a slow reentry into the everyday world. You are changed by the loss, you will not forget it, but you are beginning to be able to accommodate it and to begin to live your life as it is, without the loved person.

Grief is perhaps an unknown territory for you. You might feel both helpless and hopeless without a sense of a "map" for the journey. Confusion is the hallmark of a transition. To rebuild both your inner and outer world is a major project. Get help if you need it.

The process for each person is unique. Each person has an individual "time line." Allow yourself your uniqueness.

Distinguish between depression and sadness or sorrow. It is natural to feel great sadness for your loss. It may come in "waves" or it might be pervasive over a period of time.

You will probably have a hard time to focus or concentrate on things that feel irrelevant or unimportant. You might feel lethargic or agitated, perhaps in turns. It takes energy and attention to move through the mental/emotional process of grief and you will feel preoccupied with this psychological process.

Anger is a natural response when something you value is taken away from you.

You may feel alone, isolated or not understood.

RESOURCES FOR GRIEVING

Be aware of your body's needs for nutrition, exercise and rest. Try to listen to your body's "messages" rather than imposing what you think it <u>should</u> want to do. Listening to your body is different from "doing something for" it.
> Fear or anxiety might be expressed by shakiness or a queasy, upset stomach.
> Guilt/regrets can feel like physical burdens.
> Anger or resentment, held inside, often manifest as headaches, tight neck and shoulders, a "knotted" stomach.

Try asking the part of your body feeling a particular sensation, "If you could talk, what would you say? What would meet your need?"

Find, or create, a supportive network. These will need to be persons who are willing to listen with their hearts and to allow you to express your <u>feelings,</u> not just your thoughts.

Break any problem into or make any changes in small increments.

Feel, and try to be creative in ways to express your emotions:
> Vigorous physical exercise or work activity
> Drawing, painting or sculpting
> Writing or reading poetry
> Music or interpretive dance
> Writing a journal or an ongoing letter to your loved person
> Writing a specific letter to express anger. If you plan to edit later, or not to send it at all, you can write just as emphatically as you feel.
> Relaxation exercises, meditation, prayer, massage
> Rituals
> Shouting/screaming in your car or on an empty beach

If you are worried about depression or despair, it sometimes helps to set a time limit of perhaps an hour, by the clock or a timer. Plan a distraction for yourself at the end of the time limit. Then allow it free reign, really sink into it and, at the end of the hour, arrange the distraction you planned.

Notice the difference between feelings and mental thoughts or ideas. Both can be true even though they might be in conflict.
> "I'm glad he is no longer suffering" is true, but may conflict with the feeling of being abandoned and left to pick up the pieces of your shattered life.

Try to nurture and replenish each aspect of yourself; heart, mind, spirit and body. Take one day at a time. To look too far into the future is overwhelming and immobilizing. . . just get through today.

Sooner or later we all suffer a traumatic life event - the death of a loved one, a divorce, a job loss, a serious illness. When it happens, the rules for staying healthy and happy all change. People who suffer a trauma have to replace the resources - both internal and external - that they have lost. They must reinvent their lives.

WHAT IS TRAUMATIC

Trauma is often caused by the loss of anyone who is very important to us - a spouse, a parent, a friend, etc.

Although the loss of a relationship is the most common cause of trauma, it can also result from a loss of *productivity*...whether it's a job or an endeavor - raising children, volunteering, following creative interests, etc.

The loss of a productive outlet causes a change in our identity or role. And this makes us question who we are.

Many people think trauma is something that strikes from the outside. But traumatic problems - mid-life depression, for instance - can arise from within, as well.

HOW *NOT* TO COPE

Most people who experience a trauma feel out of control. They think their whole world is falling apart and they don't know what to do about it. It's like having a nervous breakdown. *Common no-win reactions:*

- **Feeling like a victim.** Victims sit back and say, *Look at what life has done to me.* They blame their problems on other people or organizations, and then expect to be rescued. Victims don't want to take responsibility for recovering.

- **Becoming aggressive.** You can sue the company that fired you or the hospital where a relative died. But in the end you'll get little satisfaction, and you're doing nothing to rebuild your life. Aggressors think they're acting in their own best interest. But once again, they're focusing on external forces.

BETTER WAYS

The best way to recover is to focus internally. You need to concentrate on yourself for a while. A major life crisis is a time to turn inward and challenge yourself to recover. Appraise your situation realistically. Face the fact that you are in trouble and look for ways to make even this experience useful.

Examples: A man who is in the midst of a painful divorce should ask himself what he can do to develop new relationships and be a better partner.

Different kinds of trauma require different kinds of action. . .

- **Death of a loved one.** When someone close to us dies, we confront our own mortality. We wonder why we're alive.

Helpful: Use this as an opportunity to evaluate what you are contributing to society. Look for ways to make your life better and more productive.

- **Major illness.** Although cancer and other illnesses are terrible traumas, there is much we can learn from them.

Helpful: Realize that this illness may even help you in some ways.

Example: People who have had heart attacks often start eating right and exercising for the first time in their lives. *Result:* They wind up healthier than ever.

- **Breakup of a relationship.** Although it's difficult to do, we all have to admit that there is no one relationship that can take care of us forever...we can't rely on any other person to do the things we need to do for ourselves.

Helpful: Ask yourself how you contributed to the problem - perhaps you were too needy. Look for ways you can act differently in the future. *Important:* Many people who make a healthy adjustment after a relationship fails start loving themselves for the first time.

- **Job loss.** People who lose a job immediately start redoing their resumes, reading the classified ads, networking, etc. But your first task should be to get over the trauma by taking care of yourself-eat well, exercise, get enough rest.

Helpful: Realize that it may take a year or more to find the right job and rebuild your life. Nothing good is going to happen in a hurry. See the job loss as an opportunity to get out of a rut and do something different-something you've always dreamed of doing.

Kramer, Kathryn D., "Traumatic Events Don't Have to be Traumatic," Reprinted with permission <u>Bottom Line/Personal</u>, New York, NY.

HOW TO STAY FOCUSED
AND NOT BE
DISTRACTED BY
ATTRACTIVE
DISTRACTIONS
IN THESE CHANGING TIMES

We all have things in our lives that we wish would go away - conflicts, work stress, financial woes, problem in-laws, aging parents.

The conventional way we deal with the anxiety caused by these problems is by distracting ourselves with ordinary activities - exercising, reading the paper, watching TV, shopping, talking on the phone, socializing, doing volunteer work.

Although there's nothing wrong with any of these pursuits, by carrying them to extremes we turn them into dangerously addictive distractions. And we often do this without even noticing.

Facing real problems by talking things out with the people involved or taking definitive action is scary. It's human nature to try to delay doing anything at all when a really painful problem arises.

People can fool themselves into thinking that their distractions are useful because so many of them are socially acceptable. Some distractions masquerade as very positive activities. Exercise, reading, volunteer work, socializing, etc., are all worthwhile...until they're overdone.

It can sometimes be hard to distinguish between a helpful activity and an addictive distraction. Thinking, talking incessantly about a problem, for example, can fool us into thinking we are doing something about it, avoiding confronting it.

People are attracted to distractions because they're enjoyable and they relieve anxiety. But as the time spent on a particular distraction increases, it changes from being a pleasant, anxiety reducing, intrinsically positive experience into one that's addictive. There is often time spent preparing for the activity, thinking about it and telling people about it. All this helps people to avoid their real problems.

The first step in getting rid of distractions is to find out what you are avoiding. Ask yourself: Is there anything I don't want to talk about?

LISTENING

When I ask you to listen to me and you start giving advice, you have not done what I asked.

When I ask you to listen to me and you begin to tell me why I shouldn't feel that, you are trampling on my feelings.

When I ask you to listen to me and you feel you have to do something to solve my problem, you have failed me, strange as that may seem.

Listen! All I asked was that you listen, not talk or do - just hear me.

Advice is cheap. Twenty cents will get you both Dear Abby and Billy Graham in the same newspaper.

And I can do for myself. I am not helpless, maybe discouraged and faltering, but not helpless.

When you do something for me that I can and need to do for myself, you contribute to my fear and weakness.

But, when you accept as a simple fact, that I do feel what I feel, no matter how irrational, then I can quit trying to convince you and can get about the business of understanding what's behind this irrational feeling. And when that's clear, the answers are obvious and I don't need advice.

Irrational feelings make sense when we understand what's behind them.

Perhaps that's why prayer works - God is always there, LISTENING.

So, please listen and just hear me. And, if you want to talk, wait a minute for your turn; and I'll listen to you.

Anonymous

The Chinese Characters which make up the Verb "To Listen" Tell Us Something Significant About This Skill.

EAR

YOU

EYES

UNDIVIDED ATTENTION

HEART

WHAT WE NEED DURING GRIEF

TIME: Time alone; and time with others whom you trust and who will listen when you need to talk. Months and sometimes years of time to feel and understand the feelings that go along with loss.

CARING: Try to allow yourself to accept the expressions of caring from others even though they may be uneasy and awkward. Helping a friend or relative also suffering the same loss may bring a feeling of closeness with that person.

SECURITY: Try to reduce or find help for financial or other stresses in your life. Allow yourself to be close to those you trust. Getting back into a routine helps. Do things at your own pace.

PERMISSION TO BACK-SLIDE: Sometimes after a period of feeling good, we find ourselves back in the old feelings of extreme sadness, despair, or anger. This is the nature of grief, up and down, and it may happen over and over for a time. It happens because, as humans, we cannot take in all of the pain and the meaning of death at once. So we let it in a little at a time.

REST, RELAXATION, EXERCISE, NOURISHMENT, DIVERSION: You may need extra amounts of things you needed before. Hot baths, afternoon naps, a trip, a project or "cause" to work for to help others - any of these may give you a lift. Grief is an emotionally and physically exhausting process. You need to replenish yourself. Follow what feels healing to you and what connects you to the people you love.

HOPE: You may find hope and comfort from those who have experienced a similar loss. Knowing what helped them, and realizing that they have recovered and that time does help, may give you hope that sometime in the future your grief will be less raw and painful.

SMALL PLEASURES: Do not underestimate the healing effects of small pleasures. Sunsets, a walk in the woods, a favorite food - all are small steps toward regaining your pleasure in life itself.

GOALS: For a while, it will seem that much of life is without meaning. At times like these, small goals are helpful. Something to look forward to, like playing tennis with a friend next week, a movie tomorrow night, a trip next month helps you get through the time in the immediate future. Living one day at a time is a rule of thumb. At first, don't be surprised if your enjoyment of these things isn't the same - this is normal. As time passes, you may want to work on longer range goals to give some structure and direction to your life; guidance or counseling can be helpful.

BE AWARE OF DRUG AND ALCOHOL USE: The use of drugs, alcohol, an even prescription medications may prolong and delay the necessary process of grieving. We cannot prevent or cure grief.. The only way out is through the grief process.

PERMISSION TO CHANGE YOUR MIND: Grieving can shake you up inside. You may find yourself having trouble concentrating, constantly reevaluating your priorities, or never being quite sure what you want. Let people know in advance that you may decide to change your plans.

"What We Need During Grief" was adapted from Self Help Correspondence for the Bereaved: A manual for Hospice Programs, Judith Herr, MS, Hilltop Hospice, Grand Junction, CO.

SUPPORT FOR THE WHOLE PERSON

MENTAL:

LEARN NEW SKILLS • READ NON-FICTION • UNDERSTAND PERSONAL BUSINESS MATTERS • DISCUSS IDEAS • KEEP UP ON CURRENT EVENTS • PLAN FOR MY FUTURE • EVALUATE CHOICES & MAKE DECISIONS • TEACH OTHERS • WORK PUZZLES • TAKE CLASSES • SELF STUDY

SOCIAL/EMOTIONAL

EXPRESS FEELINGS TO ANOTHER • PLAN SOCIAL EVENTS • FEEL COMPETENT • HAVE COMPANIONSHIP • LAUGH • CRY • EXPRESS ANGER • CARE ABOUT ANOTHER PERSON • FEEL CARED FOR BY ANOTHER • FEEL SENSE OF ANTICIPATION • HAVE MEANINGFUL ACTIVITY • FEEL LUCKY • FEEL APPRECIATED • FEEL ATTRACTIVE OR HANDSOME

PHYSICAL

EXERCISE • GOOD FOOD • FRESH AIR • PHYSICAL TOUCH • ENOUGH REST • TIME IN NATURE • RECREATIONAL SPORTS • REGULAR HEALTH CARE • PLEASANT HOME/WORK ENVIRONMENT • DANCING • SINGING • GARDENING • VACATION OR CHANGE OF SCENE

SPIRITUAL

PRAYER/MEDITATION • SPIRITUAL COMPANIONSHIP/COMMUNITY • FINDING PERSONAL EXPRESSION OF THE DIVINE • RELIGIOUS SERVICES/OBSERVANCES • READING SACRED/INSPIRATIONAL WRITING • FOLLOWING 12 STEP PROGRAM • AWARENESS OF HOW LIFE EVENTS AFFECT YOU THOUGHTS & FEELINGS ABOUT GOD • SHARING YOUR FAITH OR LACK OF FAITH WITH ANOTHER

PRACTICAL

RESOLVE LEGAL MATTERS • HANDLE CORRESPONDENCE • PAY BILLS • CAR REPAIRS • HOME MAINTENANCE • DECISIONS ABOUT WHETHER TO MOVE OR NOT • ARRANGE OR REARRANGE FURNITURE • DISPOSE OF BELONGINGS • HANDLE FINANCES • DO LAUNDRY • GROCERY SHOPPING • FOOD PREPARATION • HOUSE CLEANING • YARD WORK

CREATIVE

WRITING/JOURNALING • PAINTING/DRAWING • FLOWER ARRANGING • CRAFTS • PHOTOGRAPHY • DANCING • LISTENING TO MUSIC • PLAYING AN INSTRUMENT • SINGING • IMAGINING • READING FICTION/POETRY • COOKING • ATTENDING MOVIES/THEATER/BALLET/SYMPHONY • DECORATING • REALLY APPRECIATING SOMETHING (like a piece of art, a good meal, something in nature, etc.)

Source Unknown

A *cut finger-*

is numb before it bleeds,

it bleeds before it hurts,

it hurts until it begins to heal

it forms a scab and itches until

finally, the scab is gone and

a small scar is left where

once there was a wound.

Grief is the deepest wound you have

ever had. Like a cut finger,

it goes through stages and

leaves a scar.

Source Unknown

Count on Grief

By Joanette Hendel

Count on grief to increase vulnerability

Human beings are most comfortable when they are in control of their lives and circumstances. Death, even when it's expected, represents the ultimate "change in plans." When a loved one dies, our former safety and security no longer seem to exist. Instead, we may experience feelings of helplessness and vulnerability that are frightening, as well as disarming. Yet it is precisely this vulnerability that can break down walls of resistance to new thought processes and open the way for new perspectives.

Count on grief to create change

Grieving is a walk through unknown territory. Familiar internal and external stabilities disappear in a whirlwind of changing thoughts, feelings, and emotional flux. We are reminded of our pain at odd times and in unexpected ways. Emotions hover near the surface and tears are hard to control. The stress of daily living taxes our protective defenses to the limit. Depression seems to slip in from nowhere, and anger erupts without warning. Because grief requires so much emotional energy, our finesse for social game-playing is greatly diminished. The bereaved meet the world at a disadvantage, continually surprising themselves and others with unpredictable responses to familiar situations.

Count on grief to change social structure

The bereaved find their social networks changing and transforming around them. Disappointment with family and friends is a common theme. Those we expected to "be there for us" may not be able to meet our needs, and friends we didn't know we had appear "out of nowhere" to fill the void. As we come to terms with whatever limitations and expectations we have for ourselves, we also become aware of the limitations of others. Not everyone we care about will receive what they need from us while we're grieving. Not everyone who cares about us will be able to fully share our pain.

Count on grief to stress marital bond

Grief, like any other stress, complicates relationships. One grieving partner taxes a relationship - two grieving partners find their pain doubled. Because grieving is an unpredictable, moment-to-moment process, couples must be prepared to build flexibility into their union. Marriages are challenged when each expects too much from the other and neither receives adequate support from social or extended family networks. Marriages are strengthened when each partner feels supported and is allowed individuality and freedom from expectations.

Count on grief to define priorities

The bereaved often find themselves realigning their goals and objectives. For most of us, nothing is easily taken for granted after the death of a loved one. We understand that "now" is the only time there is, and that tomorrow may never come. Relationships are more precious than ever, and we are less comfortable with "unfinished business" relating to those we care about. Because the cares and concerns built into our busy lives pale in comparison to our loss, the emphasis on people versus things takes on far greater meaning.

Count on grief to increase spiritual awareness

The pain of grief prompts spiritual investigation into both the known and the unknown. Answers we were sure of before are not always satisfying in the contact of our present reality. God is questioned and religion is held up for examination. Typically, there are many stages of distancing, moving toward, and moving within old and new spiritual concepts and beliefs. Our struggle for inner peace and unity seizes many priorities. In the majority of cases, our connection to ourselves and the universe becomes far more defined.

Count on grief to strengthen compassion

Grief tears down the boundaries between ourselves and others. Bereavement enhances our humanness and strengthens our ties to the world around us. Our loss is a life-changing event; we will never again be the people we were before. Pain somehow opens us to greater levels of awareness and a greater capacity for compassion and understanding. Bereavement provides the catalyst to become more giving, more loving, and more fully aware.

Count on grief to define the past and open doors to the future

For the bereaved, the world is completely new. The death of a loved one becomes a reference point around which we define where we've been and how we structure a path for tomorrow. Grief provides a "crash course" in some of the most profound lessons life has to offer. As bereaved individuals, we find ourselves with fewer answers, but far more insights. In time, we learn there is no loss without gain and no sorrow without joy. As death closes doors behind us, new doors open before us.

From Bereavement Magazine, pp. 55-56. Reprinted with permission Bereavement Publishing, Colorado Springs, CO.

56 Presents To Give Yourself

Walk instead of ride.
Practice courage in one small way.
Give yourself a compliment.
Keep a secret.
Warm a heart.
Laugh at yourself.
Enjoy silence.
Walk to the nearest park.
Break a bad habit, if just for today.
Get to know the neighbor's dog/cat.
Hug someone.
Sing in the shower.
Walk in the rain.
List 10 things you do well.
Pay a compliment.
Throw away something you don't like.
Watch a construction crew.
Waste a little time.
Curl up before an open fire with some cocoa.
Buy a ticket to a special event.
Return something you've borrowed.
Think about droplets on a rosebud.
Try to feel another person's hurt (or joy).
Organize some small corner of your life.
Pop popcorn.
Turn off the TV and talk.
Tell someone you love him/her.
Surprise a child.
Drop a quarter where someone will find it.
Hold a hand.
Hug a tree.
Let the phone ring.
Feed the ducks.
Pick up some travel brochures & dream.
Smell a flower.
Send a card to someone for no reason.
Take an early-morning walk.
Tell someone how much you appreciate him/her.
Look into the heart of a flower.
Look at old photos.
Encourage a young person.
Follow an impulse.
Visit a lonely person.
Listen to the rain on the roof.
Acknowledge when you are wrong.
Volunteer some time to a good cause.
Give yourself a present.
Have breakfast in bed.
Let someone do you a favor.
Reread a favorite book.
Give a dog a bone.
Allow yourself to make a mistake.
Watch the sun set.
Hide a love note where a loved one will find it.
Allow yourself to make another mistake.
Take time to talk to neighborhood children.

Anonymous

BEING GOOD TO YOURSELF

Self-nurturing happens normally when you love yourself. Here are some ways you can express self-love.

Trust your heart. You know what you want and need.

Put yourself first. You cannot be there for anyone else unless you take care of yourself.

Let your feelings be known. They are important.

Value your thoughts, and let your opinions be known.

When you're angry, let yourself feel the anger. Decide what you want to do. Just feel it, express it, or take some action.

When you want something from someone else, ask. You'll be OK if they say no. Asking is being true to yourself.

When you're harassing yourself, stop. You do it when you need something. Figure out what you need and get it.

When you feel harried, slow down. Deliberately slow your breathing and take deep breaths. Slow your speech and movements.

When you feel like crying and it's not a safe place to cry, acknowledge your pain and promise yourself a good cry later. Keep your promise.

When somebody gives you a gift, say "thank you." That's all you need to do. A gift is not an obligation.

adapted from BE GOOD TO YOURSELF THERAPY; Cherry Hartman, Abbey Press 1987

SESSION THREE

FEELINGS

Session 3: Feelings

How do I cope with them?
Can I express them?

1. Send around a tablet and , if participants are willing to be called by other members of the group, ask each to list name and phone number. (While they are doing the exercise [#6], Xerox the list and distribute)

2. Overview of the session (set the "stage" for check-in)
What kinds of feelings do you experience?. . . (Answers from group)
(Display the five feeling cartoons [surprise, anger, happiness, sadness, fear] facially expressed and understood across all cultures.) (Following, pgs.90-94). One aspect about grieving that many people find very difficult is the volatile nature of the feelings. We are accustomed to being able to keep our feelings under control. It is the "out of control-ness" that gives a sense of craziness. For many people, that is scary. Our culture does not much approve of revealing feelings, especially for men. We are also at our most vulnerable when we reveal feelings. Many of us have been taught that emotions are not of equal importance with our mental and rational capacities, so our emotions become somehow shameful and we keep our feelings secret. Usually considered the *most* "dangerous" are angry and sexual feelings. Many of us have little opportunity to discover safe, satisfying ways to express them.

3. Introductions/Check-In
(Remind them this is the last session for name tags)
Give your name and the name of the person you are mourning.
Tell us how you cope with and express your feelings.
Tell us how your week was.

4. Assagioli's Seven Psychological Functions (p.99)
Holding the paper flat in the air, it is as though we are standing in the center, and the points are modes of expression, from different sources within ourselves. To feel most whole is to use, in balance, all the modes. Since grieving is *about* feelings, people often get stuck in that mode, at the expense of the others. It takes awareness and effort to bring ourselves into balance by consciously using the other modes of expression. Stimulate your mind, if you can, by directing your thoughts to areas other than your grief. Think, for perhaps 5 minutes, about politics, explore your philosophy, or think about someone else. Watch for brief flashes of wishes to do something spontaneous, and, if it's possible, *do* it. Perhaps a desire to be in a place of nurture or comfort for you (e.g. at the beach, up on Mt. Tam, shopping). Learn to access and check out feelings of intuition, see if they are trustable. If you find they are, honor them. It is here we get the sense of what is right or appropriate for us. Make time to respect the needs of your senses and know they also must be filled. Really *consider* what would taste good. What would feel good? Smell good? Sound good? Being lovingly touched is often something people miss - try a massage, allow yourself to really bask in someone's hug, take in the comfort of that.

5. Universal Grieving/Coping Model (p.57) Hand-out (p.56).

6. Exercise: Color the figure. (Following, p.95) (Provide 6-pack boxes of crayons)

You *experience* your feelings in your body, so you can see why massage feels so good to us. Or you can provide physical ways of expressing them. If, for example, you feel anger in your arms, do something physical to release the feeling - like beat on the bed or a pillow. If you feel hurt or sadness in your heart, hold something warm, like a stuffed animal or a pet, perhaps even pretend it is your loved person.

Allow time only *if* people want to share.

7. Evocative Words Exercise (List follows on pg.89)

Lay out on the floor 3X5 cards, each with a feeling or quality printed on it. Have participants notice that each has the potential for *all* of them, but we tend to use ones with which we are most comfortable, ones that come easiest. Have participants each choose 3-4 cards with feelings/qualities they want to encourage and develop. Instruct them to place the cards in a spot where they will see them often (bathroom mirror, above the kitchen sink, by the bed, etc.) "Each time you see the cards, stop and close your eyes and try to access the place where you understand and get a sense of the nature, the power of that feeling or quality. Become familiar with it, make an "easy-access" road to it and thus learn to connect and use it as appropriate occasions arise."

8. Closure

As I have heard your stories and have learned of your struggles to re-create your lives, I *appreciate* how well you have done, how hard you have tried, the obstacles you have *already* overcome. Just getting out of bed in the mornings is hard, getting through the day sometimes seems impossible, and yet you have gotten this far. You have all taken a major step toward your healing by coming into a group of strangers to try to induce the healing. Take a moment to appreciate the efforts of others in the group. . . Now take time to appreciate *yourself* for the work you have dome. . . Have a good week.

Universal Grieving/Coping Model

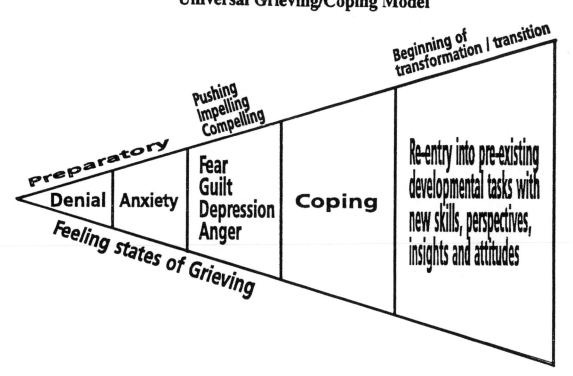

The feeling states of grieving are: denial, anxiety, fear, guilt, depression & anger, with each serving positive growth functions that help to bring feelings, thoughts, action & beliefs into congruence.

Denial and anxiety serve to prepare the bereaved person for the change task that lies ahead.

Denial buys time to discover the inner strengths, and to assemble the external supports needed to face the facts, conclusions, implications and feelings associated with the loss.

Anxiety first mobilizes, then focuses the energy needed to enact the internal and external changes imposed and demanded by the impact of the loss.

Fear, guilt, depression and anger push/impel the person to make profound internal and external changes that the loss demands.

Fear facilitates re-commitment to attachment, to loving, in spite of the vulnerability, sense of abandonment and pain brought on by the loss.

Guilt facilitates resolution of the basic existential question, "Of what meaning, significance or impact are my feelings, thoughts, actions, or beliefs on the important events or occurrences in my life? Does it matter?"

Depression acts as a medium for redefining competency, capability, value and potency, concepts that are violated by core level loss. They are personally defined, often by the Wounded/Injured Child. Embittered, self-hating or define new criteria?

Anger Acts as a medium for redefining one's sense of universal fairness and justice, a sense often violated by the impact of a profound loss

The coping process is the behavioral enactment of the philosophic changes that grow out of the grieving process.

No prescribed order to the feeling states.

Dr. Ken Mosely (workshop)

Universal Grieving / Coping Model

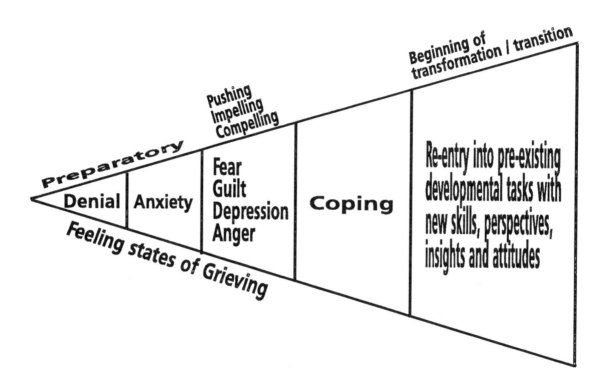

The Interpersonal Costs of Anger

While anger can sometimes feel relieving, and while it can act as a powerful tool for influence or control, anger has a price. It takes a toll on your relationships and costs you in support and satisfaction. The price is often loneliness and isolation. Chronic anger-induced isolation also affects you physically, making you more susceptible to disease.

Angry people are experienced as dangerous. They are handled like a loaded gun - with caution or downright avoidance. Anger stuns. It frightens. It makes people feel bad about themselves. It makes people put on their emotional armor as soon as they see you. The more anger you express, the less you are heard, and the more cut off you may begin to feel from closeness. The more you behave aggressively, the angrier you become. Anger-fueled aggression cuts and scars the tissue of relationship. Angry relationships spawn an atmosphere of vigilance and fear. Your energy gets channeled into erecting barriers rather than into communication and problem solving. The barriers defend you against hurt, but they also make it impossible for angry people to reach each other.

Angry people often express a sense of helplessness. Anger leads to helplessness in four simple steps:

1. You tell yourself, "I'm in pain, something is wrong or lacking."
2. You tell yourself, "Others should fix or provide it." The angry person puts responsibility on others to meet his basic needs, giving up his own power.
3. You express your anger with aggression.
4. Your anger is met with resistance and withdrawal, you feel frustrated and #1 repeats.

The angry person feels his life slide out of control. Nothing seems to work. No one really cares. No one seems good enough.

Adapted from **When Anger Hurts,** by Matthew McKay PH. D., Peter D. Rogers, PH. D., Judith MCKay, R.N. New Harbinger Publications, Inc. 1989

Alternative Stress-Reduction Strategies

Anger is just *one* of many coping strategies to discharge stressful arousal. Any one of the following can be used *instead of anger* when you are stressed.

- Crying: helps discharge tension/discomfort, relaxes tight muscles, helps communicate your needs.
- Exercising
- Intense physical work activity: vacuuming, painting, fixing, building
- Humor, fun, silliness
- Writing: poetry, journal writing
- Relaxation exercises
- Verbalizing pain: shouting in your car or on an empty beach or to someone else
- Recreation: reading, TV, games, hobbies act as psychological sponges to sop up stress
- Problem-solving activities: dealing with the root problem, you anticipate relief and you feel less helpless.
- Problem-solving communication
- Pillow and bed beating
- Music
- Resting: even brief periods like counting or taking a deep breath before making a response

Self-destructive strategies:

- alcohol and drugs
- recklessness and danger seeking
- compulsive sex
- taking the helpless/victim position

Why You Choose Anger to Reduce Stress

Three factors influence the choice of any stress-reduction strategy:

- Physiological predisposition (constitutional tendencies, neurological wiring)
- Family conditioning (reinforcement for behaviors)
- Social learning (acquired through modeling, imitation of parent(s))

Adapted from **When Anger Hurts**, by Matthew McKay, PH. D., Peter D. Rogers, PH.D., Judith McKay, R.N., New Harbinger Publications, Inc., 1989

RAGING

WHAT TO DO WITH ANGER

Bottling up anger can create a host of health problems; *venting* anger can wreak havoc on relationships and can have attendant health consequences, as well.

In one study, for example, University of Michigan researchers studying anger found that people who brooded had the highest blood pressures, people who "blew up" had the second highest, and people who took steps to resolve their anger had the lowest blood pressures of anyone.

The following tips may help if you're prone to bottling things up or blowing up.

- **Consider making a list of things you're angry about.**
  If you feel a vague, non-specific anger toward your job, your boss, a relative, etc. writing down *what/whom* you're angry at, and *why* you're angry can help you clarify the problem so you can take steps to solve it.

- **Rethink the situation.**
  Instead of bottling up or blowing up when someone says something "unkind," cuts you off in traffic, or foists a last minute job upon you, take a moment to rethink the situation. If you can tell yourself that the person is probably having a bad day (we all have our bad days), there's a good chance you won't get angry. See if you can work on *empathizing* with the person, instead of judging him.

- **Ask yourself how you feel.**
  When you're hot, hungry, tired, or headachy, you're more apt to become hot under the collar than when you're feeling good. Try not to say anything to anyone until you've had something to eat, gotten some sleep, taken a shower, etc.

- **Watch out for "shoulds."**
  Often we get angry because people don't act like they *should* act, or because situations don't happen the way the *should.* Anger dissolves when we realize that there is no reason why other people should live up to our standards, or why things should happen the way *we* think they should happen.

- **Laugh.**
  Transforming an injustice into an absurdity is one way of rethinking a situation. It's hard to get angry and laugh at the same time.

- **Exercise.**

  A feeling of being cooped up or caged in can ruffle the calmest of personalities. Whether the "cage" is a small workspace or the responsibilities of parenthood, some brisk exercise can work wonders in offering a feeling of release. The physiological stress response (tightened muscles, pounding heart, excess adrenalin, etc.) - the result of the "Fight or Flight" reaction - also can be dissipated through brisk exercise.

- **Discuss It.**

  A "let's stay calm and let's consider how we might deal with this problem" approach is not only healthful, but constructive. The trick here is to explore the problem in a *detached* manner and not to allow it to upset you. Energy is focused on problem-solving rather than on arguing.

Reprinted with permission
"Raging," HOPE Health Publications, Kalamazoo, MI

THE OAK AND THE REED

An Oak, which hung over the bank of a river, was blown down by a violent windstorm. As it was carried along by the river, one of its boughs brushed against a Reed which grew along the shore.

The Oak was filled with admiration and could not help asking the Reed how he came to stand so erect and undamaged after such a severe storm--a storm that had torn up an Oak by its roots.

"There is no great secret in this," replied the Reed. "I secure myself by a conduct that is the reverse of yours: instead of being stiff and stubborn, and being proud of my strength, I yield and bend to the winds. I let the storm pass over me, knowing how fruitless it would be to resist."

MORAL:

A person of a quiet, still temper - whether it be given him by nature or acquired by art - calmly composes himself in the midst of a storm, so as to elude the shock, or receive it with the least detriment.

He is like a prudent, experienced sailor who, in swimming to the shore from a wrecked vessel in a swelling sea, does not oppose the fury of the waves, but stoops and gives way that they may roll over his head.

The doctrine of absolute submission in all cases is an absurd dogmatical precept...but, upon particular occasions, and where it is impossible for us to overcome, to submit patiently is one of the most reasonable maxims of life.

-Adapted from *Aesop's Fables* (published 1818)

To acknowledge & express emotions, keep a diary/journal:
(to track what tips off feelings)

Date	What I was Feeling	Situation	What I was Thinking

SESSION FOUR

RITUALS

Session 4: Rituals
What are they?
How can they help me?

1. Overview
    Change or transition is always scary and feels dangerous because it is the unknown, it is unpredictable, it is uncharted, something you haven't done before. Societies and religions recognize this feeling of danger by creating formalized, structured expression for it (e.g. rites of puberty to adulthood, marriage, christening/baptism. The Jewish tradition has the whole first year of mourning structured by events through time.) Our own culture has, to a great extent, questioned rote rituals and has abandoned many of them.

    The ritual of remembrance which, of course, comes first to mind is the funeral or memorial service. But this is definitely not the last or the only ritual you can use. You probably incorporate rituals in your life without calling them that—perhaps a nightly time of dialogue with your loved person before you go to sleep, perhaps a flower or candle placed beside his picture, maybe an evening toast or a bow of respect to his container of ashes or playing a particular piece of music on a regular basis. Journal-writing (perhaps in the form of an on-going letter to your loved person) can be viewed as a ritual.

2. Introductions/Check-in (no name tags)
    Give your name (to help us remember without name tags)
    Give the name of the person you're mourning
    For your check-in, tell us what, if any, rituals you find helpful in your life.

3. Rituals create the context and the container for expressing a feeling. Feelings, like sadness for example, are often all-pervasive, from horizon to horizon. Rituals bring in, focus and express the feeling. They give opportunity for focused connection. They create a receptivity as well as an out-pouring of emotion. You can identify a feeling and create a ritual to express it.

    There are three areas in which our relationships can be emotionally incomplete (p.). You might create a ritual to complete any one of them A ritual is especially helpful to complete with someone who has died.
    a. **Making amends:** things we are sorry for having done or said or *not* having done or said, and resolving to do it better next time. Regrets, not guilt: we are *human!* To regret means you are sorry, guilt implies you are shameful, not a good person.
    b. **Offering forgiveness:** things we need to forgive others for *and* to forgive ourselves for.
    c. **Expressing** significant emotional statements that we need or want to say (e.g. I love you, I'm proud of you, I thank you—things we perhaps took for granted)

4.   Exercise: Collages
Gather a collection of pictures with potential symbolic content (e.g. scenes from nature, animals, people, activities, events, etc.) from magazines, newspapers, brochures, etc.

Spread them out on a table and instruct:
a. Choose 5-6-7 pictures that appeal to you, ones which attract you or "speak" to you. (While they are choosing, put on each chair an 11"X14" sheet of paper and a glue stick.)
b. Return to your chair and paste the pictures on the paper in any configuration you want.
c. When complete, each shares the collage.

In a subjective, right-brain mode of "seeing," you will probably be able to discern a "theme" in each collage. Notice the colors (vibrant or cool or a combination?), the action/vitality vs. serenity/peace?, the quality or "home," the subjects represented. Often the collages will be arranged to represent two themes in balance (e.g. sadness and hope, light and dark) and often the participant will speak of this him/herself. Make what comments you can about each, or ask a question to clarify. If, for example, the collage includes all peaceful scenes from nature, perhaps ask if s/he can find the place within where that quality of peace is. Or ask what it represents to the person him/herself.

(Participants can also do this exercise at home with photographs. Some might have done it for memorial service.)

5.   Closure: (Ritual to acknowledge our mutual needs and inter-relatedness)
Distribute small pieces of paper & pencils. Have each write his/her name and phone # and fold the papers twice (so all look the same). Collect them in a small basket and have each choose a folded paper.

Instruct: All you have to do is think of the person whose name you drew as many times a day as you can: think healing, loving, compassionate thoughts, wish him/her well in his/her day.

You can, if you want, call, meet for dinner or whatever you want. Also take particular notice of how it feels to you to know another person is doing this for you.

Mail postcards requesting participants bring "rituals objects" to the next meeting. Mail early enough so they have 2-3 days to decide what to bring.

* *

Grief Support Group for <u>Day, Date</u>

You probably have something which symbolizes your loved one's essence- an object which represents him, something which represents something you did together or symbolizes your life together, something which sums up the feelings you have experienced. Bring one thing or a group of several objects to group next week--perhaps a picture, a poem, art work, a letter or whatever you feel is appropriate. You will be asked to describe their meaning during the group.

This is another form of ritual, the subject we discussed last week.

RITUALS

Create/Design your own ritual
- A ritual is a specific behavior that gives symbolic expression to certain feelings/thoughts.
- Basic purpose is to provide a structured way to recall the deceased, acknowledge the loss, express feelings/thoughts about him and allow the memory to continue.
- Decide what you want to express and find a behavior that can convey this.
- May be done once or many times.
- May be formal/informal.

Suggestions for rituals/symbols:
- Buy a flower
- Burn a candle
- Plant a tree
- Choose someone needy to occupy the empty chair
- A special Christmas ornament
- Give a donation in your loved one's name
- Bring out a special possession representing the loved one
- Assign a special role to someone else (e.g. "pass the torch")

Therapeutic properties of rituals:
- The power of acting out. The physical ritual act touches on unconscious feelings more effectively than words.
- Permission for emotional & physical expression: acceptable outlet for feelings, symbols to focus on.
- The delimitation of grief. Ritual = distinct beginning and end with clear purpose (vs diffuse, global reactions), feelings more manageable.
- Channel for grief feelings or complete unfinished business.
- The opportunity to "hold on" to your deceased loved one without doing so inappropriately or interfering with your grief work: the chance to interact intensely with the memory.
- Provides experience to recognize & confirm loss.
- Collective rituals allow participation of family/friends.
- Rituals tap into or confront anniversary reactions, not always recognizable.

Adapted from Grieving: How To Go On Living When Someone You Love Dies, Rando, Therese A., Macmillan Publishing Company, 1988

RITES FOR THE DEAD

1. All transitions are experienced as dangerous, none more so than the transition from alive to dead.

2. Through ritual a society acknowledges the psychological danger of transitional states. By providing socially acceptable forms, such rituals help to contain and limit expression of emotions, without having to deny or repress them.

3. The ritual helps reduce a sense of confusion or disintegration. It offers a structured, formal expression. It gives a sense that there is available a weight of social experience and knowledge for individual orientation and guidance to reduce a sense of helplessness and isolation.

4. Death rituals seem to provide form and expression for the many ambivalent feelings involved when someone dies.
   a. Sadness at the loss
   b. Guilt
        1) that one has perhaps contributed to the death
        2) that the 'other' is dead while we are still alive
   c. Anger at the 'abandonment'
   d. Dread of death for oneself, awareness of mortality

5. Through the death rites, the living can feel they are still connected with the dead. The living can be of service by providing what the dead seem to need, help them find their way in their new world, intercede with the spiritual powers on their behalf.

6. Finally the death rites help the mourners come back to life and to re-integrate into the social community.

Adapted from Dying and Creating: A Search for Meaning, Gordon, Rosemary.
Society of Analytical Psychology LTD., 1978

CREATE A RITUAL TO COMPLETE UNFINISHED AREAS

The only three areas in which we can feel emotionally incomplete:

1. *Making Amends* - things that we're sorry for either having said or done, or not said or done.
   * We can be sorry for not having acknowledged a positive event. We can also be sorry for our part in creating a negative event.
   * Making amends is saying you're sorry *and* being willing to change your behavior, backing it up with action.

2. *Offering Forgiveness* - things we need to forgive others for, either real or imagined.
   * You have some erroneous beliefs - so has everyone else.
   * You've made mistakes - so has everyone else.
   * In order to forgive yourself, you must forgive others.
   * Forgiving people does not mean endorsing their actions. Forgive the mistakes/emotionally or mentally ill *part* of the person.

3. *Expressing Significant Emotional Statements* - that we need or want to say. (e.g. "I love you, " "I thank you," "I was proud of you," etc.
   * The wife asks, "Do you love me?"
   * The husband responds, "Didn't I buy you that new coat?"
   * She asks about apples and he talks about eggs.

Make a list for all three categories.
Then, for each item on the list, what would it sound like if you had a chance to say it?
Keep it simple.

Examples:
"I forgive you for the time you lied."
"I'm sorry I didn't trust you."
"I never told you how important all the little things were."

THOUGHTS

We shall not cease from exploration
And the end of all our exploring
Will be to arrive where we started
And know the place for the first time

> T. S. Eliot: *Little Gidding*

What we call the beginning is often the end
And to make an end is to make a beginning.

> T. S. Eliot*: Little Gidding*

As early as 1930 and 1931 Jung had written of death
as an essential constituent of life. In his paper, "The
Stages of Life" (1930), he remarked:

> As a doctor I am convinced that it is hygienic to discover
> in death a goal towards which one strives.

And in 1931 in *The Secret of the Golden Flower*,
he wrote:

> Death is psychologically as important as birth and, like
> it, is an integral part of life.

"Memories are like stars in the dark
night of sorrow. Time shall soften
the pain until all that remains is the
beauty of the memories...and the love
- *always* the love."

(Author Unknown)

SESSION FIVE

SUPPORT SYSTEMS & THE STRESS OF BEREAVEMENT

Session 5: Support Systems and
The Stress of Bereavement
What are my needs for support: How & where do I get it?
What are the stresses I experience: How can I ease them?

The sharing of "ritual objects" takes a long time (1-1 1/2 hrs.), it is very moving and awesome and therefore difficult to change the pace to discussion of stress. Use the Overview time for discussion of support systems and stress and rely on hand-outs to give more in-depth information.

* *

1.   Overview
The "fight or flight" response is a physical solution for danger. It served our early ancestors well for survival of the species, but modern man's saber-toothed tigers are often emotional. There are many times in the day for each of us where it is not appropriate or possible to either fight or flee: an angry encounter with a supervisor, a traffic snarl, the bus doesn't come on time, delivery of the wrong item. Notice that often these occasions are the result of unfulfilled expectations.

The body, however, doesn't distinguish between physical and emotional danger and does its age-old thing to prepare us:
- Heartbeat ↑ (more blood to muscles)
- Breathing rate ↑ (more oxygen to the blood)
- Blood sugar elevates
- Muscle tense (prepare for action)
- Blood is sent to the upper muscle & legs, taken from other body sections not on emergency demand (e.g. digestion ceases)
- Muscles of bowels/bladder constricted or released for greater mobility
- Hyper-vigilance
- Adrenaline pumps into the bloodstream

You can imagine the effect on your body if all this happens 2, 8, 19 times a day without any way to discharge by fight or flight. Among other things, excessive experience of stress harms our immune system,

Stress is created in a 3-step process.
    a. The event in the environment (over which we have little or no control)
    b. Our mental interpretation of it (*Thinking* creates our experience of reality)
    c. The emotional response to the interpretation

How to help:

A few deep breaths (easy to do anytime, anywhere)

"Let go" of stress-makers: change your mental interpretation

Physical exercise

Hypnosis/meditation/biofeedback/guided imagery

Support system

Let people know what you need

Support of different _kinds_ may have to come from different _sources_ (emotional, mental, spiritual, practical)

Cultivate those people who fill your needs

2. Sharing of "ritual objects." Allow as much time as each wants to talk. These are precious and cherished pieces of the "together time" and group members are very vulnerable as they share them. Great need for gentle understanding.

3. Closure:

Our hearts are warmed and touched by the privilege of sharing these memories of your together-time. Our feelings are tender toward each other as a result of the sharing. We feel close to each other and to all the absent ones. Go with blessings and feel each other's caring during the week.

I Think I'm Having
STRESS!!

Typical Stress-Producing Beliefs in our Culture

1. It is a dire necessity for an adult human being to be loved or approved of by virtually every significant other person in his community.

2. One should be thoroughly competent, adequate and achieving in all possible respects if one is to consider oneself worthwhile.

3. Certain people are bad, wicked or villainous and they should be severely blamed and punished for their villainy.

4. It is awful and catastrophic when things are not the way one would very much like them to be.

5. Human unhappiness is externally caused and people have little or no ability to control their sorrows and disturbances.

6. If something is or may be dangerous or fearsome, one should be terribly concerned about it and should keep dwelling on the possibility of its occurring.

7. It is easier to avoid than to face certain life difficulties and self-responsibilities.

8. One should be dependent on others and need someone stronger than oneself on whom to rely.

9. One's past history is an all-important determinant of one's present behavior and that, because something once strongly affected one's life, it should indefinitely have a similar effect.

10. One should become quite upset over other people's problems and upsets.

11. There is invariably one right, precise and perfect solution to human problems and it is catastrophic if this correct solution is not found.

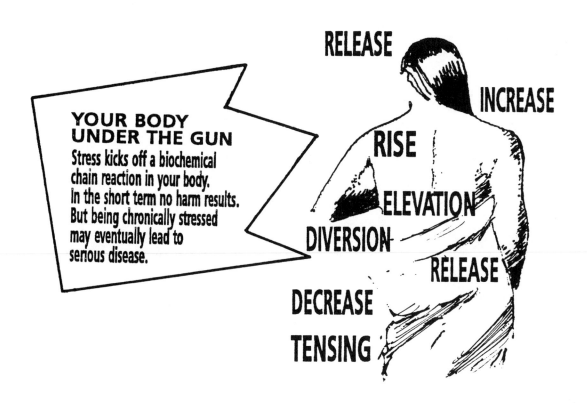

YOUR BODY UNDER THE GUN
Stress kicks off a biochemical chain reaction in your body. In the short term no harm results. But being chronically stressed may eventually lead to serious disease.

RELEASE of energizing fight-or-flight hormones
INCREASE in brainwaves boosting alertness; pupils dilate
RISE in breathing rate, preparing the body for action
ELEVATION of heart rate and blood pressure
DIVERSION of blood cools the skin
DECREASE in blood flow to stomach; stomach acid rises
RELEASE of fat and cholesterol into the blood by the liver
TENSING of muscles, readying you to fight of flee

When you're under stress, your body undergoes several biochemical changes that can have a profound effect on you health, with chronic stress over time. First, the adrenal glands pump out the hormones "adrenaline" and "cortisol." Together, these hormones raise your heart rate, blood pressure and blood flow; your breathing rate increases to push extra oxygen into your muscles, which also tense. (This prepares your body for physical action: fight or flight.) Blood glucose (sugar) is diverted form your internal organs to your brain to increase your alertness. Perspiration increases and blood is diverted to reduce body temperature. Most bodily functions not vital to fighting or fleeing - such as digestion - are temporarily suppressed. Finally the body releases "endorphin," a natural tranquilizer that brings the hormone levels back down to normal.

WHAT MAKES PEOPLE "STRESS RESISTANT"?

Six Characteristics

of stress-resistant people, helpful for managing life stress and thus decreasing anxiety, depression and physical illness.

√   They take some **personal control,** "reasonable mastery" over their world. They realize they can't control everything, but these people begin by identifying a problem and gathering information they need to help them solve it. That may mean speaking to others, reading, drawing on life experience - and developing some strategies. They choose which they think is best, implement it and then evaluate it. If it doesn't work, they go to the second or third strategy. If they begin to see a pattern where nothing is working, they rethink the problem, and perhaps find there is nothing they can do about it. They have the ability to accept that none of us can control everything.

√   Stress-resistant people are **committed to seeing something through to completion -** "task involvement." This could be completing a college education, a community project, getting ahead in, or changing a career; these people have something to live for instead of day-to-day boredom.

√   They make certain **healthy lifestyle choices.** That includes minimizing stimulants like caffeine and nicotine, since both those chemicals produce the physiology of the life-style choice of finding a way to relax every day - even just 10 or 15 minutes a day. It can range from exercise to meditation to relaxation, music, art, hobbies, or just sitting quietly. These people also choose some form of aerobic exercise for the heart muscle - jogging, swimming, etc. They do it for 20 minute periods three times a week, not only reducing the physiology of stress, but keeping it at a lower level.

√   They **seek out social support.** The literature seems to indicate that social support strengthens and stabilizes cardiac response, lowers blood pressure and strengthens the pulse. A caring social support system also strengthens the immune system's capacity to fight disease, as well as circulating more endorphins, the body chemicals which produce feelings of calm and well-being.

√   The fifth characteristic is **humor.** People who can play, or be with those who can make them laugh are better able to cope with stress. Humor helps us to keep things in perspective. It's also largely a right-brain activity, which reduces stress.

√   The sixth characteristic is **concern for the welfare of others.** The concern could find expression in getting involved in a community project, care-giving, service to others. There is some evidence of a genetic component for stress-resistance, but these skills can also be learned.

Adapted from work by Dr. Raymond Flannery, Assistant Professor of Psychology, Harvard Medical School

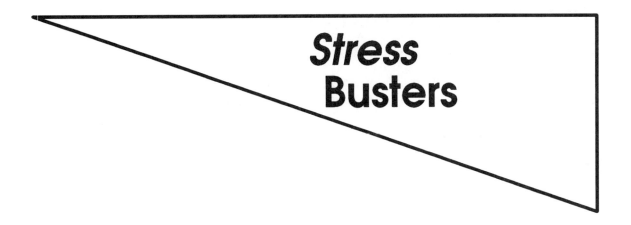

Stress Busters

8 *Spot Tension* RELIEVERS

- Feeling tired and drawn? A hand massage is a good revitalizer. Massage the inside of your right hand by making circular motions in the palm with the thumb of your left hand. Work your way across, from thumb to pinkie. Then massage each finger, gently pulling upward as you go. Give special attention to the joints. Repeat on left hand.
- Use this same technique on your feet: Massage the arch, ball of the foot, toes, heel and Achilles tendon.
- You can help a headache by squeezing your right hand. Here's how: To locate the pressure point on your right hand, place the ball of your left thumb on the back of your right hand, over the web between the thumb and forefinger. Now gently squeeze the web, using your left thumb and your left fingers. Continue the pressure for several moments or until your headache disappears.
- Another headache remedy: Place one hand, palm-side down, over the area on you head where you feel the most pain. Put the other hand across the back of your neck at the base of your hairline, and simultaneously press both points.
- To relax stiff muscles, first tighten, then release them. (Works well in the neck and shoulder area.)
- Raise shoulders to ears for a few seconds, lower and release.
- Clench fists tightly, hold for several seconds, release and repeat.
- Another technique to try the next time you feel paralyzed with anxiety: Close your eyes and take a mini vacation. Visualize a beach scene - rolling waves, sparkling water, palm trees in the wind - gradually, you'll clam down and return to reality feeling refreshed.

HOT TIP: The good news about bad news. One of the reasons you feel calm after crying is that it gives your respiratory, circulatory and nervous systems a good workout.

Breathing LESSONS

Relieving stress can sometimes be as simple as taking a deep breath. Stress causes quick, shallow breathing that can lead to increased tension. Adjusting your breathing may help your relax.

- Sit in a comfortable position, placing your palms on your thighs. Shift your concentration away from your problems by focusing completely on your body. Take a long, *deep* breath.
- Allow your diaphragm, not your chest, to fill completely (your stomach will protrude), and hold for a count of three.
- Slowly exhale and tell your body to relax,
- Feel the soles of your shoes on the ground and your toes inside.
- Begin mentally working your way up the body, at each point acknowledging spots of tightness or tension.
- Be aware of your muscles and bones from the tip of your toes to the top of your head.
- Feel your back, shoulders, head and neck against the chair. Repeat until you feel relaxed.

HOT TIP: When your stomach's upset, try placing a cold washcloth on your tummy. The coolness of the temperature acts as a temporary tranquilizer and dissolves the knots.

5 Sure Stress REDUCERS

Here are a few simple practices that may make your life a little less stressful (*Methods compliments of The Hope Heart Institute, a nonprofit research organization*):

- **Save time.** Prepare for the hectic morning the evening before by setting the breakfast table, making lunches and pressing clothes for the next day.
- **Disconnect it.** Want to take a long bath, meditate, sleep, or read without interruption? Unplug you phone for an hour.
- **Never leave home without one.** Be prepared to stand in line with a paperback or favorite magazine. Reading can make almost any wait nearly pleasant.
- **Forget about counting to 10.** Count to 1,000 before doing something or saying anything that could make matters worse than they already are.
- **Get up and stretch.** If your job requires you to sit for long periods of time, stand up and reach for the ceiling.

Reprinted with permission, "Stress Busters," The Family Circle, New York Times, Co., New York, NY

BURN-OUT OR STRESS SYMPTOMS

* Feeling unable to slow down and relax

* Explosive anger in response to minor irritation

* Anxiety or tension lasting more than a few days

* Feeling that things frequently go wrong

* Inability to focus attention

* Frequent or prolonged boredom

* Fatigue

* Sexual problems

* Sleep disturbances

* Tension headaches

* Migraine headaches

* Cold hands or feet

* Aching neck and shoulder muscles

* Increased consumption of alcohol

* Indigestion

* Menstrual distress

* Nausea or vomiting

* Loss of appetite

* Diarrhea

* Ulcers

* Heart palpitations

* Lower back pain

* Allergy or asthma attacks.

* Constipation

* Shortness of Breath

* Frequent colds

* Frequent low-grade infections

* Frequent minor accidents

* Overeating

* Increased dependence on drugs

Meditation

Relax in just 20 minutes

Meditation is the art of focusing your attention so completely on one thing that you lose consciousness of everything else around you.

Although meditation often is associated with religious disciplines, modern researchers have found that it can be used apart from any religious or philosophical orientation to promote deep relaxation and mental stillness.

4 Things that help

1. **A quiet environment**
    Find a place where you won't be disturbed (unplug the phone and put a "Do Not Disturb" sign on the door). It is helpful to try to meditate in the same place everyday; eventually you will begin to associate this place with relaxation.

2. **A comfortable position**
    It is *not* necessary to sit in a straight-back chair or on the hard floor in a lotus position. Find a comfortable, upright chair that you can sit in for 20 minutes without stress on your back or legs. (Don't choose a recliner or you'll probably fall asleep.)

3. **A word to still your thoughts**
    In order to still your internal stream of thoughts, it's necessary to choose a word (or phase) to repeat mentally. Good words to choose for repetition end in an *m* or *n* sound, such as *calm, home,* or *shalom.*

4. **A passive attitude**
    Although there is some work involved in collecting your wandering thoughts and concentrating your attention on repeating your chosen word, it is essential that you otherwise remain passive. Don't think about how you are feeling. Don't "watch" yourself becoming more relaxed.
    With practice, your concentration will become so complete that you'll find your whole body is numb when you first open your eyes after meditating.

WHAT HAPPENS DURING MEDITATION?

University studies have shown that, among other things, heart rate, respiration, and blood pressure drop, and that *alpha brain waves* - the brain waves associated with *deep* relaxation - increase in intensity and frequency. *Blood lactate,* a chemical associated with anxiety, has been found to fall rapidly within the first ten minutes of meditation.
Several studies have shown that people with hypertension can reduce their blood pressures (all day) after committing themselves to a regular routine of 20 minutes of meditation, morning and evening.□

"The nice thing about meditation is that it makes doing nothing quite respectable."

How to meditate

- Sit up right in a comfortable chair

- Close your eyes as in sleep. (There should be no tension on the eyes or on your forehead.)

- Take a few minutes to relax your whole body. Shake your shoulders, inhale and exhale deeply and slowly a few times, and clear your mind of thoughts and concerns.

- Begin mentally repeating your chosen word - over and over, very slowly. Pour your *full* attention into this repetition. The objective is to repeat your word without a break so that outside thoughts do not enter your mind. When you discover that your mind has left off the repetition and has begun wandering about, simply pull it back in and continue with the repetition. (Note: don't become discouraged when your mind wanders; refocusing your attention on the repetition is part of the meditative process.)

- Try to remain as still as possible during meditation. If you feel the need to scratch an itch, try ignoring the need and focusing on the repetition; your itch should go away. If you really feel as if you must change your position slightly or scratch, do so, then resume meditating.

- You may find it difficult to sit perfectly still and focus your attention for more than five or ten minutes when you first start out. With daily practice, however, you should be able to work up to 20 minutes of meditation, twice a day. (Before breakfast and before dinner - when your stomach is empty and you are alert - are recommended times for meditation.)

Reprinted with permission HOPE Health Publications, International Awareness Center, Kalamazoo, MI, "Relax in just 20 Minutes,"

AIDS-RELATED
STRESS AND BURN-OUT

SELF ASSESSMENT

This form is designed for professional caregivers (including health care providers, social workers, counselors, ministers, volunteers) who care for persons with AIDS. It is designed to help you:

° recognize symptoms of stress

° identify which aspects of your work you find most stressful

° take action to prevent burn-out

Check the items that reflect your personal experience and needs. Each person's responses will be unique. Some items may have particular significance for you. You may want to circle or underline those areas of particular concern and note where some action or change might assist you in more effectively coping with the stress of AIDS care.

KAIROS Support for Caregivers:

114 Douglass Street
San Francisco, Ca 94114
(415)-861-0877

84

SYMPTOMS OF STRESS

Physical

I have been experiencing:

_____Frequent colds   _____Headaches   _____Indigestion
_____Lethargy   _____Insomnia   _____Fatigue

_____ _____   _____ _____   _____ _____

Emotional

I have been feeling:

_____Sad   _____Exhausted   _____Angry
_____Frustrated   _____Overwhelmed   _____Confused
_____Resentful   _____Depressed   _____Anxious
_____Helpless   _____Inadequate   _____Alienated

_____ _____   _____ _____   _____ _____

Coping

I am concerned about:

_____Eating more   _____Smoking   _____Sleeping more
_____Drinking   _____Withdrawing   _____TV watching
_____Drug use   _____Carelessness   _____Isolation
_____Workaholism   _____Compulsiveness   _____Obsessiveness

_____ _____   _____ _____   _____ _____

KAIROS Support for Caregivers

114 Douglass Street
San Francisco, Ca 94114
(415)-861-0877

Self-Assessment:
AIDS-Related Stress and Burn-Out

SOURCES OF STRESS

The aspects of Aids Caregiving that I find most stressful:

Internal (Personal needs, expectations, values, feelings)

_____Fear of getting disease   _____Gays with AIDS
_____So many dying   _____Drugs users with AIDS
_____Young people dying   _____Women with AIDS
_____Unpredictable symptoms   _____Infants with AIDS
_____Discussions of suicide   _____Co-workers with AIDS
_____Not having a cure   _____Friends with AIDS
_____Not knowing what to say   _____AIDS-Related Dementia
_____Dealing with families   _____My own HIV status
_____No one to talk to   _____Fear of my own death

_____ _____   _____ _____

External (Other's needs, expectations, work environment)

_____Demanding patients/clients   _____Lack of information
_____Demanding supervisors   _____Lack of public support
_____Insufficient staff   _____Legal/ethical issues
_____Staff turnover   _____Constant policy changes
_____Staff absenteeism   _____Poor communication
_____Out-dated equipment   _____Low morale
_____Long hours   _____Agency "politics"
_____Paperwork   _____ _____

Identify the stress factors over which you may have some control by getting information and/or taking action (e.g. finding someone to talk to; requesting training, cutting back on hours, changing assignments, etc.

KAIROS Support for Caregivers

114 Douglass Street
San Francisco, Ca 94114
(415)-861-0877

PREVENTING STRESS

Recent research identified the following coping strategies among professionals effectively coping with the stress of AIDS care giving:

° **AWARENESS**

How can I tell when I am experiencing stress? What conditions and situations do I find stressful?

° **ATTITUDE**

What am I seeking in my work? How can I "let go?" Where can I say "no?"

° **SUPPORT**

What kind of support do I need?

___Coping with stress   ___Listening to patients   ___Alcohol/drug issues
___Recognizing my limitations   ___Laughing more   ___Difficult patients
___Ethnic/cultural issues   ___Dealing with grief   ___Spiritual concerns
___ _____

The best way for me to get that support is:

___One-to-one   ___Class   ___Training Materials
___Support Group   ___Workshop   ___ _____

° **RESPITE**

How can I "take breaks" from stressful situations?

___Meditation   ___Weekend getaways   ___Leave of absence
___Daily breaks   ___Vacations   ___ _____

° **EXERCISE**

What non-competitive activity would help me release tension?

___Walking   ___Swimming   ___Hiking   ___Dancing
___Running   ___Aerobics   ___Gardening   ___ _____

° **SELF-NURTURING**

What can I do for myself?

___Adequate sleep   ___Home Environment   ___Hobby
___Balanced Diet   ___Social Activities   ___ _____

List all the things you like to do; do at least one each day.

AREAS OF POSSIBLE STRESS

DEALING WITH BILLS

ANSWERING CORRESPONDENCE

DIFFICULTY EATING/SLEEPING

ADAPTING TO CHANGES

FAMILY/FRIENDS

QUESTIONING FAITH

EMOTIONAL "ROLLER-COASTER"

MENTAL CONFUSION

WORRY

LONELINESS/ISOLATION

DIFFICULTY TO FOCUS/CONCENTRATE

LEGAL PAPERWORK (estate, wills, etc.)

FINANCIAL CONCERNS (not enough money)

NOT ENOUGH EXERCISE

LOSS OF INTIMACY/CLOSENESS

NEW HOUSEHOLDS RESPONSIBILITIES

GEOGRAPHICAL CHANGES

LOSS OF SAFETY/SECURITY

HOLIDAYS, ANNIVERSARIES, BIRTHDAYS

LOSS OF INTEREST IN NEWS/WORLD EVENTS

GENERAL DECISION-MAKING

WITHDRAWAL FROM RELIGIOUS/SPIRITUAL
PRACTICE

Exercise: Evocative Words

admiration, appreciation, attention
balance, beauty, bliss, brotherhood
calm, compassion, comprehension, cooperation, courage, creativity
daring, decisiveness, detachment, determination, discernment, discipline
endurance, energy, enthusiasm, eternity
faith, freedom, friendship
generosity, goodness, gratitude
harmony, humor
inclusiveness, infinity, initiative, integration *
joy
liberation, light, love
order
patience, peace, persistence, positiveness, power
quiet
reality, renewal, resoluteness
serenity, silence, simplicity, synthesis, spontaneity
tenacity, truth
understanding, universality
vitality
wholeness, will, wisdom, wonder

Adapted from The Unfolding Self, Molly Young Brown 1983 Psychosynthesis Press.

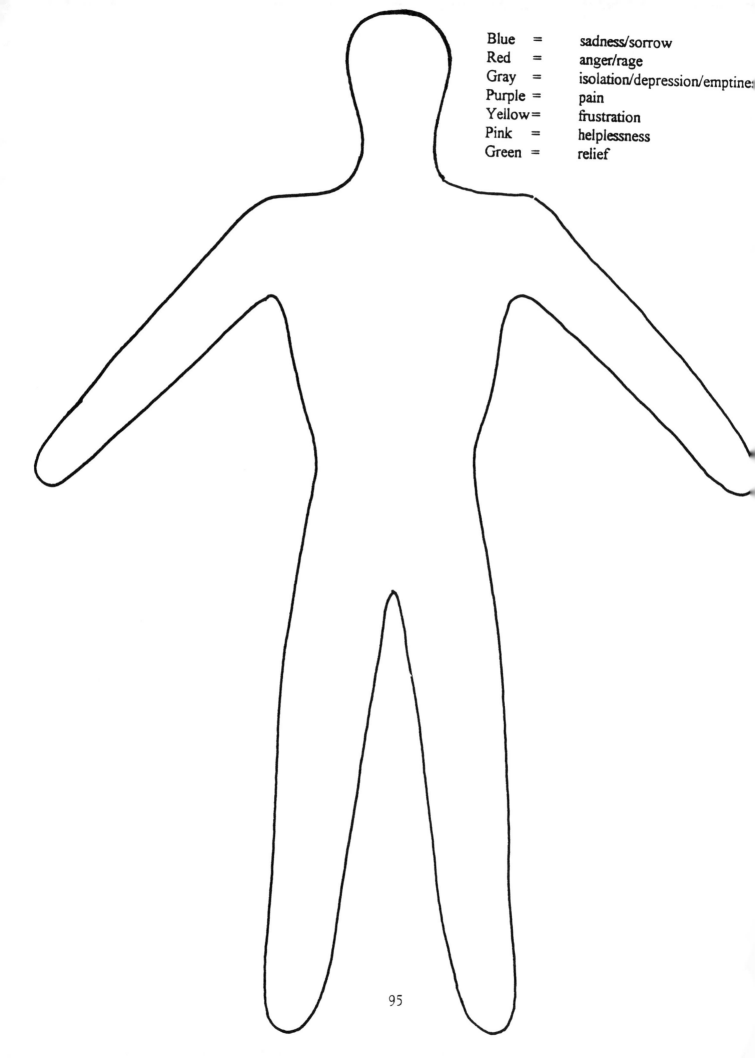

Blue   =   sadness/sorrow
Red   =   anger/rage
Gray   =   isolation/depression/emptiness
Purple   =   pain
Yellow =   frustration
Pink   =   helplessness
Green   =   relief

95

ANGER

Anger makes us feel righteous, but not happy
It may or may not be the right or the real issue

The Function of Anger
The sole function of anger is to stop/reduce/discharge the arousal generated by stress.
You are in pain and are trying to do something about it. Anger does this by discharging or blocking awareness of painful levels of emotional or physical arousal.
Four kinds of stress dissipated by anger:

1. **Painful affect.** Anger can block off painful emotions so that they are literally pushed out of your awareness. It can discharge high levels of arousal experienced during periods of:
   * anxiety & fear
   * loss & depression
   * hurt
   * guilt & shame
   * feelings of failure, badness & unworthiness

2. **Painful sensation.** Stress is often experienced as a physical sensation:
   * "Relieve pain by anger."
   * Muscle tension (most common form, usually gathers in forehead, jaws, shoulders & abdomen)
   * Pressures of rushing
   * Physical pain
   * Over stimulation
   * Fatigue, Overwork

3. **Frustrated drive.** Anger functions to vent stress from the frustrated, blocked drive to achieve something you need or want.
   * The blocked struggle to have what there isn't enough of
   * Things are not as they should be; frustration to one's picture of order, oughtness, perfection
   * The sense of being forced

4. **Threat.** Any perceived threat to your physical or psychological well being generates a strong push for some stress-reducing activity.
   * Feeling physically threatened by illness
   * Feeling attacked
   * Feeling engulfed, controlled
   * Feeling abandoned (for child, a threat to survival)

How You Create Anger

Anger is a 2-step process:

1. Starts with stress and its generated experience of arousal, motivates you to begin coping to reduce or block the uncomfortable feelings. 1st step concludes when awareness of stress leaks to a coping decision. Stress by itself is not a sufficient cause for anger. Anger-triggering thoughts are needed to convert stress into hostility.
2. Process of focus on either "blamers" or "shoulds."
   "Blamers:" You deliberately did _____ to me. Intentional harm by the wrong behavior of another.
   "Shoulds:" You should not have _____, but instead you should have _____. The person knows, or should know, how to act correctly but has stupidly or selfishly broken the rules.

Both kinds of trigger thoughts have, as a core belief, a perception of the other person as bad, wrong & deserving of punishment.
   Stress + trigger thoughts = anger.

The Anger Cycles

Feedback loops:
1. Stress/arousal → Trigger thoughts (the most common)
2. Trigger thoughts → Arousal/stress
   In cycle 2, there is always an intervening moment of pain between the trigger thought and the anger, but the perception that the pain is someone else's fault ignites the anger

loss	fear
rejection	frustration
despair	hurt
abandonment	

Adapted from When Anger Hurts by Matthew McKay, Ph. D., Peter D. Rogers, Ph. D., Judith McKay, R.N.
New Harbinger Publications, Inc., 1989

FEELINGS

If we want to be loved we must reveal ourselves. If we want to love someone they must allow us to know them.

As obvious as this may be, many of us go through life avoiding such disclosure. In fact, most of us practice concealment by playing roles. We claim to have certain feelings which we actually do not have, we profess to be loving when we're full of hostility, calm when in reality anxiety is nearly overwhelming us, and to believe in things when in truth we do not.

Even with those persons we care about we share little of our true feelings, beliefs, or needs. Perhaps because we want to be loved we fear the truth that may come with openness and consequently we present ourselves as the sort of person we believe would be accepted and loved - and we attempt to hide the things we think would damage that image.

Another reason we try to conceal ourselves is the fear of change. For most people change is frightening and we want to think of ourselves as "constant." We've molded our image and seem to believe we are all that we ever could be when in reality our needs, desires, goals, values, behavior and feelings change with experience and age.

Still another reason we fail to expose our real self is that we don't really know how. We've never been taught how. In fact, we learned more about how to conceal our true identity, the result being that we continue to accept and play our roles. Our society encourages us, in fact, pressures us to suppress all of the emotions and characteristics that it considers "unacceptable." Of course, there are times when honest leveling isn't possible and role-playing is appropriate in the social system we must be a part of and which requires certain discipline. The key is "appropriateness" - to be private when we wish, but also able to be honest and open, without fear. We are human beings, alive, always growing and full of feelings - feelings that may be labeled "comfortable" or "uncomfortable" - "pleasant" or "unpleasant" but not "good" or "bad." Feelings are perhaps our most personal possessions and when they are not managed appropriately they can be devastating. We must be able to identify our feelings, accept them as an integral part of us and manage each one as it comes, avoiding suppression when possible, and then go on to the next feeling, for with certainty, it will come.

Author Unknown

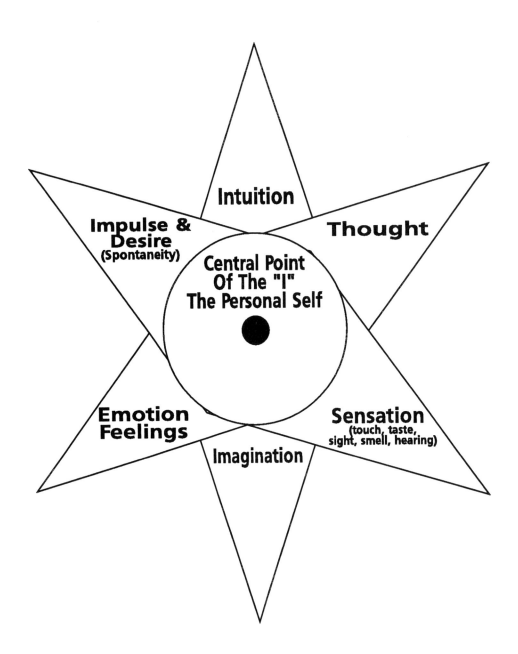

Assagioli: Seven Psychlogical Functions

The self is a system (like a family)
The self is equal to more than the sum of its parts

Permission from David Bach, Berkshire Center For Psychosynthesis

Grief Feeling Responses

_____Sadness

_____Confusion

_____A feeling of abandonment

_____A feeling of powerless, loss of control, helplessness

_____Fear that seems to have no origin

_____Anger at God/Fate; anger at the unfairness of the world

_____Anger toward self; anger toward the deceased

_____Guilt for being alive

_____Guilt for doing or not doing something

_____Guilt for not being good enough

_____Guilt for inheriting something

_____Guilt for feeling relieved

_____Auditory or visual hallucinations

_____Depression

_____Difficulty concentrating or focusing

_____Memory losses

Positive Self-Talk
'AS YOU THINK, SO YOU BECOME'

The extent to which we love and respect *ourselves* has a lot to do with how well we relate to the world around us and, consequently, with how much "stress" there is in our lives.

Following is a list of *affirmations* for building self-esteem. The way to use affirmations is to repeat them to yourself so frequently that you start believing them and *living* them.

Consider taping this list to your bathroom mirror and reading it once through before work, or taping it over your desk so it's handy all day. Or, you can take *one* affirmation *each* day, memorize it, and repeat it to yourself during spare moments - so it really sinks in.

Taking Charge: affirmations for building self-esteem

1. I am a valuable and unique individual, and I am worthy of the respect of others.
2. I look at life/I am learning to look at life optimistically and I am eager to accept new challenges.
3. I am/I am learning to be kind, truthful, patient, and compassionate.
4. I am/I am learning to be optimistic about reaching my goals. I look at temporary setbacks as stepping stones to strengthen character and resolve.
5. I enjoy/I am learning to enjoy receiving compliments, and I enjoy helping others get recognition and credit for the work they do.
6. I feel/I am learning to feel warm, loving, and good about myself.
7. I am not affected/I am learning not to be affected by the negative opionions of others; I enjoy giving my best, growing in awareness, and striving to live up to my own high standards.
8. I am successful to the extent that I feel loving toward myself.
9. There is no one in the world who is more important than I am; there is no one who is less important.
10. Every day I make time to count my blessings.
11. I am/I am learning to be productive and efficient; I divide big jobs into manageable ("bite-size") tasks, and I do one thing at a time.
12. I am/I am learning to be gentle, forgiving, and kind to myself.
13. I do not/I am learning not to worry. If something can be done about a problem here and now, I do it; otherwise, I let go of it.
14. I appreciate/I am learning to appreciate every moment of my life. I don't dwell on the dead past or the imagined future.
15. I love/I am learning to love everyone unconditionally, including myself.
16. I understand/I am learning to understand everyone and everything around me as my teacher.
17. I understand that to be upset over what I *don't* have is to waste what I *do* have.

Reprinted with permission, HOPE Health Publications, Kalamazoo, MI

RESPONDING TO FEELINGS

EFFECTIVE

- Accept support via hugs, physical touch

- Accept support through talking, expressing feelings, telling my story

- Developing inner resources

- Cry & talk with friends as needed

- Steady involvement with work

- Physical activity, exercise

- Taking care of self: eating, sleeping, nurture

- Contemplation, prayer, search for meaning

- Seek professional help

- Learn through experience of suffering

- Receptive to new ways of being & thinking: choices

NOT SO EFFECTIVE

- Relying on friends, external resources

- Overactivity

- Emotional repression; depression, volatile mood changes

- Physical symptoms: pounding heart, empty/upset stomach, fatigue, trembling, appetite loss

- Restless, unable to concentrate

- Overindulgence: increased eating, drinking, smoking

- Anger/blaming and/or guilt

- Thoughts of suicide, of "running away from it all," feeling of overwhelm

- Isolation

- Rejection of friends/relatives

- Denial of changed reality

- Intense feeling of preoccupation

- Abuse of drugs, Rx or others

IT'S TIME TO

Dr. Edward DeBono
International Center for Creative Thinking

We all think many different kinds of thoughts -- from positive to negative and everything in between. One way to become a better thinker is to separate these different kinds of thinking and use each one separately, instead of in a jumble, as we usually do.

I do this by assigning six *imaginary* hats -- each a different color -- to the different types of thoughts. By pretending to put on a hat, you can focus your mind on one particular type of thinking.

HOW IT WORKS

One of the biggest traps in thinking is that we categorize people according to *type*. This limits people to expressing views that are expected of them.

Example: Someone who is identified as a negative personality is always expected to come up with negative ideas.

By pretending to switch hats, everyone can come up with a wide spectrum of thoughts on the same subject. Wearing the hats also helps overcome ego--another big hang-up in thinking.

Example: If a person opposes an idea, he/she usually won't look for any points in favor of it. But if he's wearing a positive thinking hat, it becomes a game to find the positive side.

This gives people the freedom to remove their egos from the thinking process and think in many different ways.

MY SIX HATS

- *White hat:* **Objective Thinking.** *Memory jog:* White...Paper...Neutral...objective.

   While you wear the white hat, you concentrate on the facts. You can also point out any gaps in the information. White-hat thinking does not involve arguments, views or opinions.

- *Red hat:* **Feelings.** *Memory jog:* Red...fire...anger (seeing red)...emotions.

   While you wear the red hat, you can express hunches and intuitive feelings. You may not be able to explain your feelings...they may be based on experiences you can't put your finger on.

   In many discussions - particularly in business - we're not supposed to include our feelings. But we put them in anyway...disguised as logic. The red hat lets us express our feelings openly.

   Example: A head of research at DuPont often asks for three minutes of red-hat thinking at the start of a meeting. He wants to know how everyone feels about a project...without having to explain or justify their feelings.

   Telling someone, *You've got your red hat on,* is a way to let him know he's expressing his feeling when he's trying to be objective.

- *Black hat:* **Caution.** *Memory jog:* Black...gloomy...negative...the color of a judge's robe.

   While wearing the black hat, you can think about logical negatives - why something is illegal, why it won't work, why it won't be profitable, why it doesn't fit the facts or experience.

   Although some people get the impression that black-hat thinking is bad, it's at least as useful as any of the other kinds of thinking.

   Black-hat thinking can be used as a way to get people to *stop* being negative. *Good statement:* That's great black-hat thinking...but now let's try our green hats.

- *Yellow hat:* **Logical, positive thoughts.** *Memory jog:* Yellow...sunny...positive.

   While you wear the yellow hat, you *must* be logical.

   Example: A family is considering moving to the country. Yellow-hat thinking involves looking at logical considerations - lower housing costs, better schools, etc. Just saying that it would be nice to have a change is red-hat thinking.
   Note: The black and yellow hats are both judgment hats. *Black says:* Let's look at the difficulties and dangers. *Yellow says:* Let's look at the feasibility, benefits and savings.

- *Green hat:* **Creativity.** *Memory jog:* Green...grass...fertile growth...energy.

   While you wear the green hat, you're free to generate new ideas, alternatives and possibilities.

   Example: A couple planning a vacation puts on their green hats and brain-storms possibilities--the wilder the better. These aren't ideas they've checked or thought seriously about...they're just ideas.

   Normally when we're discussing something, it's very difficult to slip in creative ideas. Wearing the green hat is a way of making off-the-wall ideas acceptable.

- **Blue hat:** **Objective overview.** *Memory jog:* Blue...cool...the color of the clear sky, which is above everything else.

While you wear the blue hat, you tell yourself or others which of the other five hats to wear. It's like conducting an orchestra.

Blue-hat statement: We haven't gotten anywhere by being logical. Putting on my blue hat, I suggest we have some red-hat thinking to clear the air.

The blue-hat says: Let's look at our objectives and values. It lets you lay out your goals, evaluate how far you've gotten, summarize the results and reach a conclusion.

HOW TO USE THE HATS

You can use the hat concept to think about any issue. You can use it by yourself, with one other person or in a group.

Good statements:
- Let's try some green-hat thinking for three minutes to generate some different ideas.
- It seems you're just wearing your black hat...why don't you take it off now?
- That's all red-hat thinking...we need to put on our white hats for a while and consider the facts.
- Putting on my black-hat, I want to talk about the difficulties, dangers and problems we might face with this.
- Wearing my red hat, this is how I feel about it.
- Here's a provocative idea I got while wearing my green -hat.

To stimulate creativity at a meeting, ask every one to put on his green hat for three minutes and come up with some creative ideas. This will allow even the most unimaginative member of the group to indulge his creative side. *Note:* Make it a rule that anyone can call for some green-hat time.

Make it feel like a game to get people to play along. If everyone else is wearing a yellow-hat, someone who's still expressing black-hat ideas is going to feel very silly.

Make sure that every idea that is brought up is analyzed under each hat. Once you've narrowed your options down to three or four, go back and do one more yellow-black-hat check on each. At the end of this process you will have a well-thought-out plan of what you want to do.

Reprinted with permission
"Its Time to Think, Think, Think," by Dr. Edward DeBono. Bottom Line/Personal, New York, NY.

How Do You Feel Today?
PART I

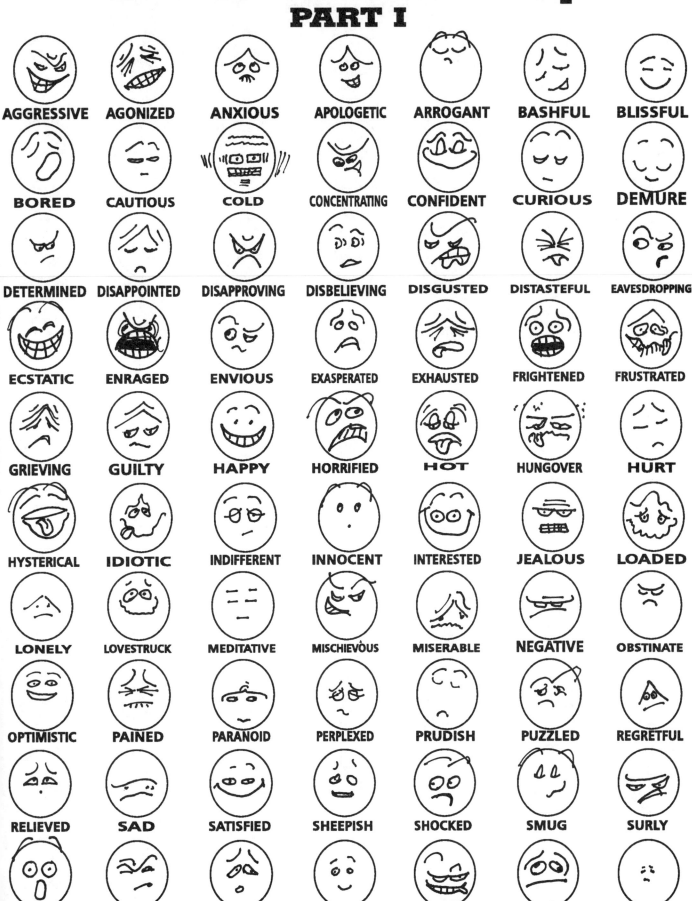

AGGRESSIVE	AGONIZED	ANXIOUS	APOLOGETIC	ARROGANT	BASHFUL	BLISSFUL
BORED	CAUTIOUS	COLD	CONCENTRATING	CONFIDENT	CURIOUS	DEMURE
DETERMINED	DISAPPOINTED	DISAPPROVING	DISBELIEVING	DISGUSTED	DISTASTEFUL	EAVESDROPPING
ECSTATIC	ENRAGED	ENVIOUS	EXASPERATED	EXHAUSTED	FRIGHTENED	FRUSTRATED
GRIEVING	GUILTY	HAPPY	HORRIFIED	HOT	HUNGOVER	HURT
HYSTERICAL	IDIOTIC	INDIFFERENT	INNOCENT	INTERESTED	JEALOUS	LOADED
LONELY	LOVESTRUCK	MEDITATIVE	MISCHIEVOUS	MISERABLE	NEGATIVE	OBSTINATE
OPTIMISTIC	PAINED	PARANOID	PERPLEXED	PRUDISH	PUZZLED	REGRETFUL
RELIEVED	SAD	SATISFIED	SHEEPISH	SHOCKED	SMUG	SURLY
SURPRISED	SUSPICIOUS	SYMPATHETIC	THOUGHTFUL	TURNED-ON	UNDECIDED	WITHDRAWN

106

How Do You Feel Today?
PART II

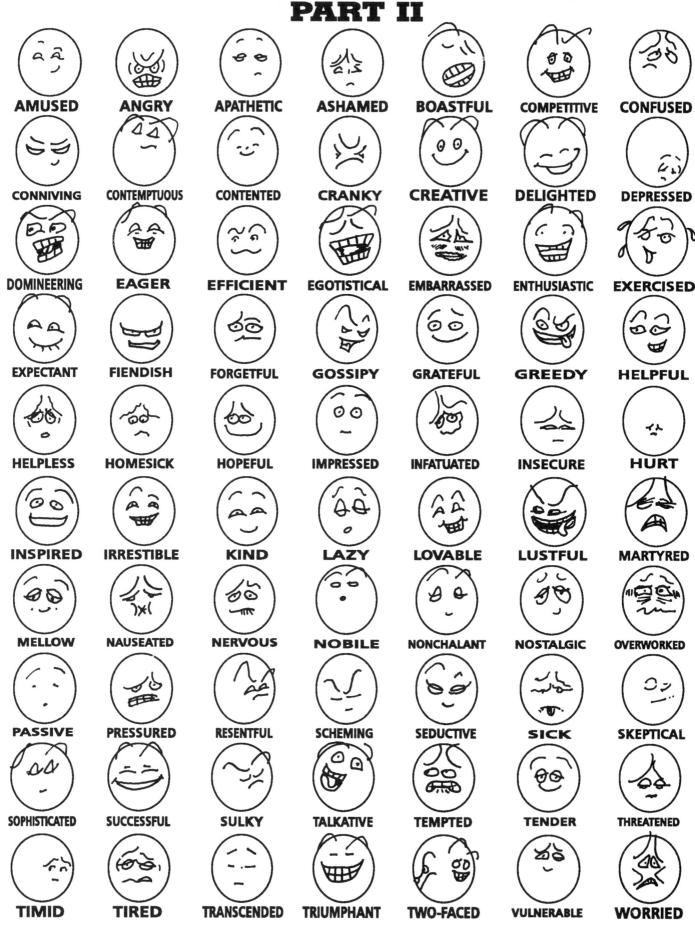

AMUSED	ANGRY	APATHETIC	ASHAMED	BOASTFUL	COMPETITIVE	CONFUSED
CONNIVING	CONTEMPTUOUS	CONTENTED	CRANKY	CREATIVE	DELIGHTED	DEPRESSED
DOMINEERING	EAGER	EFFICIENT	EGOTISTICAL	EMBARRASSED	ENTHUSIASTIC	EXERCISED
EXPECTANT	FIENDISH	FORGETFUL	GOSSIPY	GRATEFUL	GREEDY	HELPFUL
HELPLESS	HOMESICK	HOPEFUL	IMPRESSED	INFATUATED	INSECURE	HURT
INSPIRED	IRRESTIBLE	KIND	LAZY	LOVABLE	LUSTFUL	MARTYRED
MELLOW	NAUSEATED	NERVOUS	NOBILE	NONCHALANT	NOSTALGIC	OVERWORKED
PASSIVE	PRESSURED	RESENTFUL	SCHEMING	SEDUCTIVE	SICK	SKEPTICAL
SOPHISTICATED	SUCCESSFUL	SULKY	TALKATIVE	TEMPTED	TENDER	THREATENED
TIMID	TIRED	TRANSCENDED	TRIUMPHANT	TWO-FACED	VULNERABLE	WORRIED

107

Source Unknown

The Angry Victim Syndrome

We think of victims as weak, powerless people
who can easily be taken advantage.of
...but some victims aren't weak at all

By Dr. Martin G. Groder

Some victims are strong-willed people who get angry when they can't control others.

These people, whom I call *angry victims,* want others to live up to their often unreasonable expectations...and then feel angry when people inevitably disappoint them.

In order to change, angry victims have to realize that the problem lies within themselves, and that controlling others is not the solution.

WHO'S AN ANGRY VICTIM

Angry victims, most of whom are women, swing between two poles--the desire to control...and the desire to please.

Example: When Laura disagreed with her husband, she would first suppress her anger in order to please him. Eventually, however, she would swing to the control pole and fly into a rage. But then, she would start to worry about losing him...and backpedal, apologizing profusely for getting so angry. *Result:* He became confused and the relationship ultimately suffered.

Angry victims constantly flip back and forth in their emotions because they're not comfortable in either mode. They're afraid that if they exert too much control, people will become distant and angry with them.

At the same time, they're afraid that if they try too hard to please , people will take advantage of them.

Whichever pole they gravitate to, they're *afraid* of something...and sure to lose no matter what they do. *Result:* Angry victims live in a state of constant fear.

Since pain hurts more if you're already fearful and tense, angry victims are often stunned by the depth of the feelings generated by a minor disappointment. A normal domestic problem can seem like a tragedy.

Example: Len's wife, Nora, got tied up at the office one night. She came home late and forgot to call. Len felt rejected and flew into a rage.

Although angry victims expect a lot from their friends and loved ones, most have a limited tolerance for the expectations and desires of others. This allows them to blame others for their problems.

Example: Sue, who hadn't had a serious relationship in years, finally met a man who appeared to be perfect for her...but two months later, she was complaining about him. For one thing, he dropped in whenever he wanted to, which she thought was rude and demanding. After some counseling, Sue realized that she hadn't had a relationship for so long because she didn't want to put up with anyone else's schedules. The problem was hers, not his.

ARE YOU AN ANGRY VICTIM?

There are three aspects to the angry victim syndrome:
- •Fear of abandonment.
- •Fear of engulfment.
- •Need to control.

If you suspect you're an angry victim, give yourself these test:

•**Abandonment test.** Fantasize that everyone in your life calls you on the same day and says they never want to talk to you again. How much rejection would it take - one person, two people, 10 people-for you to feel devastated?

If even one rejection would be extremely hurtful, you're probable trying too hard to please people.

•**Engulfment test.** Fantasize that everyone in your life calls you on the same day and invites you out to dinner. How many offers would it take to make you uncomfortable?

Again, the fewer people it would take, the more likely it is that you're afraid of being overwhelmed with a lot of love and attention.

•**Control Test.** Think back to minor disappointments, when people who you depended on did something that you thought was wrong. What was your reaction to those incidents? Did you laugh or cry or get angry?

If you got angry or frustrated, you probably have a control problem. And the sooner you felt that way, the bigger the problem.

HOW TO STOP BEING AN ANGRY VICTIM

If the above test shows that you could be an angry victim, follow these steps:

•**Go easy on yourself.** Most angry victims are extremely self-critical. Don't beat yourself up because you've discovered the problem - understanding that you have a problem should be the first step toward overcoming it.

•**Realize that your expectations are *not* unnatural.** They come from our bedrock fears about the world - that we're not going to be loved and cared for...that we can't control what happens to us.

Instead of rejecting these fears, be aware of them and be honest about them... with other people as well as with yourself.

•**Let others know how you feel.** Talking things over with people you're close to is the best way to work out your angry-victim problems.

Example: Jody was upset because her friend Tina never seemed to have enough time for her. She fought the desire to get angry and told Tina how she felt. Tina explained that her idea of friendship was having a lot of casual friends to see occasionally for lunch. Although the two couldn't be close friends, the conversation helped Jody break out of her angry-victim cycle.

•**Recognize when you're out of balance.** Work to stay in the *golden zone--* where you feel adequately loved yet adequately free to do what you want and reasonably in control of your life.

This is a very hard balance to maintain, and you won't get there by pushing yourself. *Better:* Respect and acknowledge your needs for love, freedom and control.

Reprinted with permission
"The Angry Victim Syndrome," Dr. Martin Groder, Bottom Line/Personal, New York, NY.

LETTING GO

HOLDING ON

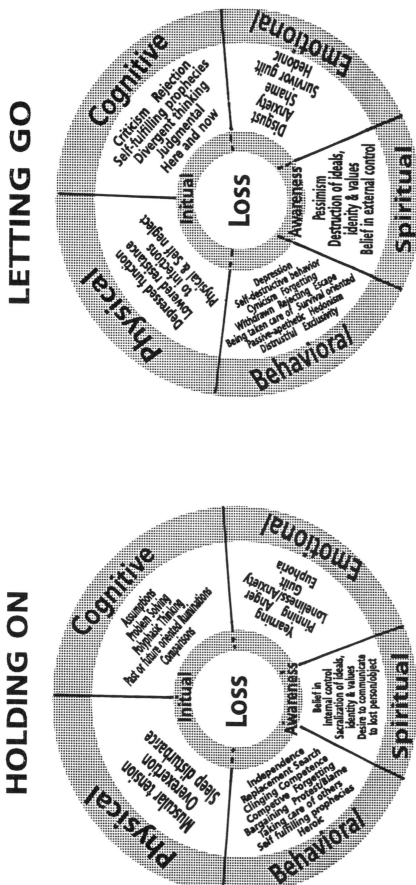

Attempts to limit awareness, to limit the impact of loss. A search for an alternative to grieving

"HOLDING ON" (Fight) ← Often Interchangeable → "LETTING GO" (Flight)

The intent is to find some way to prevent, overcome or reverse the loss.
It is usually based on the individual's belief that if he/she just tries hard enough, anything can be overcome.
"It's best not to dwell on it. Keep busy."

The intent is to conserve energy, to minimize the significance of the loss and thus, the grief.
Usually centered in belief in helplessness.
Protective; to keep from feeling overwhelmed. Respite.
"I don't want to talk about it. It doesn't do any good."

111

THE SOCIAL READJUSTMENT SCALE

LIFE EVENT

	LIFE EVENT	POINT VALUE	YOUR SCORE
1.	Death of a spouse	100	_____
2.	Divorce	73	_____
3.	Marital separation	65	_____
4.	Detention in jail or other institution	63	_____
5.	Death of a close family member	63	_____
6.	Major personal injury or illness	53	_____
7.	Marriage	50	_____
8.	Fired at work	47	_____
9.	Marital reconciliation	45	_____
10.	Retirement	45	_____
11.	Major change in the health/behavior of a family member	44	_____
12.	Pregnancy	40	_____
13.	Sexual difficulties	39	_____
14.	Gain of a new family member (e.g., through birth, adoption, mother moving in, etc.)	39	_____
15.	Major business readjustment (e.g., merger, reorganization, bankruptcy, etc.)	39	_____
16.	Major chance in financial status	38	_____
17.	Death of a close friend or family member (other than spouse)	37	_____
18.	Change to a different line of work	36	_____
19.	Major change in the number of arguments with spouse (more/less than usual regarding child-rearing, personal habits, etc.)	35	_____
20.	Taking out a mortgage/loan for a *major* purchase (home, business, etc.)	31	_____
21.	Foreclosure of mortgage/loan	30	_____
22.	Major change in responsibilities at work (promotion, demotion, lateral transfer, etc)	29	_____
23.	Son or daughter leaving home (through marriage, attending college, etc.)	29	_____
24.	Trouble with in-laws	29	_____
25.	Outstanding personal achievement	28	_____
26.	Spouse beginning or ceasing work outside the home	26	_____
27.	Beginning or ceasing formal schooling	26	_____
28.	Major change in living conditions (building a new home, remodeling, moving, etc.)	25	_____
29.	Revision of personal habits (dress, manners, etc.)	24	_____
30.	Trouble with your boss	23	_____
31.	Major change in working hours	20	_____
32.	Change in residence	20	_____
33.	Change in schools	20	_____
34.	Major change in usual type/amount of recreation	19	_____
35.	Major change in church activities (a lot more/less than usual)	19	_____
36.	Major change in social activities (a lot more/less than usual)	18	_____
37.	Taking out a loan for a *lesser* purchase (for car, TV, freezer, etc.)	17	_____
38.	Major change in sleeping habits (a lot more/less than usual, change in part of day when you sleep)	16	_____
39.	Major change in family get togethers (a lot more/less than usual)	15	_____
40.	Major change in eating habits (more/less, different meal hours or surroundings, etc.)	15	_____
41.	Vacation	13	_____
42.	Christmas/Holiday season	12	_____
43.	Minor violations of the law (traffic or jaywalking ticket, disturbing the peace citation)	11	_____

Source: Adapted from Holmes, Th & Rahe, RH: "The Social Readjustment Rating Scale." Journal of Psychosomatic Research 11:213-218, P. 125. Permission to reprint given by HOPE Health Publications, Kalamazoo, MI.

GOING AFTER LAUGHTER

1. Do something different - Eat with your opposite hand, etc.

2. Create a humor environment - Ha Ha bulletin board, funny signs...

3. Diffuse anxieties by preparing alternative humorous responses to stress situations.

4. Experiment with jokes - Learn one a week and spread it around. (jokes, however are only a small part of humor)

5. Laughter is contagious - Hang around others who make you laugh.

6. Conscious effort - Write down & file things that amuse you.

7. Focus humor on self - After you've used up all the funny things about yourself you can move on to others.

8. Share troubles - Laughter and tears are cathartic.

9. Seek the child within - It's still there wanting to play.

10. Be around children - They are some of our greatest teachers.

11. Be positive - Find someone doing something right, or almost right, and *tell* them about it.

12. Keep FUN-raising items handy - Toys, signs, posters, etc..

13. Intimidated? - Draw cartoon of person afraid of; make as outrageous as possible...or see person on toilet.

14. Give fun gifts - Garage sales often have great inexpensive items.

15. Can't laugh? Smile! Can't smile? Fake it!

16. You are not becoming a comedian - You are seeking humor for balance & perspective.

17. Dress-up - Halloween, April Fool's Day, Mad Hatter's Dinner Parties are great for this.

18. Schedule play time - If you don't, it won't happen.

19. Waste some time - Type A behaviors don't know how to do nothing.

20. OK to be silly - When things get too serious, sometimes nonsense makes the most sense.

21. Look for opportunities in the negative. They're always there!

22. Practice. Practice. Practice.

SESSION SIX

FINDING MEANING IN LOSS

Session 6: <u>Finding meaning in Loss</u>

Have I learned anything from this experience?
How will this loss affect my life?

1. Overview

Since time began, mankind has been searching for meaning, life-purpose, a plan, a structure or a framework to make some kind of sense of existence. There has always been a need to create some kind of order out of chaos, meaning out of seeming randomness.
Is Someone, Something, Anything in charge?
A Universal Life Force, Supreme Being, a single God, a pantheon of gods?

* For the American Indians, Nature created a cyclic order
* For the ancient Greeks, it was a pantheon of gods who were capricious and human like

2. Check-in

Tell us, if you want, about your own search for meaning, or just tell us how your week went.

3. Grief is provoked not just by the loss of a relationship itself, but by the disintegration of the whole structure of meaning centered around it. Your friends, your job, your activities of daily living, your purchases, your pet - all have their meaning in the <u>context of the relationship</u> - and the loss changes everything.

Depression=loss of meaning (Schiff)

Children's sense of security depends on attachment to the particular nurturing figure they recognize as their own. Attachment is overwhelmingly important to a child in its earliest years. It underlies all our understanding of how to survive in and manage our world. Attachment is so central to our security in childhood, that is becomes embedded, ineradicably, in the meaning of safety and reward for the rest of our lives. Bereavement, therefore, because it robs us of a crucial attachment, profoundly disrupts our ability to experience life as meaningful and our ability to organize experience in a meaningful way.
(Adapted from "Grief, Loss of Meaning and Society," Peter Marris, BA)

So, as a result of the loss, we ask ourselves (perhaps unconsciously) such questions as:
* How do I relate to the world?
* Who am I in the world?
* How do I fit in the scheme of things?
* What is my meaning or purpose?

A loss calls into question:
   * Our spiritual faith (or lack of)
   * Our style of behavior which is based on:
   * Our core/fundamental beliefs: Does loss fit into my belief scheme?
      Is my belief system conditioned, for example, by the maxim, "If I'm good, I will be rewarded"?
   * Our expectations: Do my expectations fit with existence as I know it? The Buddha spent much time and reflection on man's suffering and determined a major cause to be unrealistic expectations or understandings.

4. Exercise
   Distribute pads of paper and pencils.
   To fully understand an episode in my own story, I must wait for the ending. (Stuart Charme)
   a. So, think back, call back in your memory a past loss in your life, perhaps loss of a job, moving to a new place, loss of a friend, perhaps another death. . .
      What about the event was the loss? What did the loss represent to you?. . .
      What did you learn? Did you resolve to do anything differently the next time?. . .
      What happened if you tried the "doing differently"? Was it effective?. . .
      Did your life change as a result of that loss?. . .

   "There are many ways of breaking a heart. Stories are full of hearts broken by love, but what really broke a heart was taking away its dream - whatever that dream might be."
   -Pearl S. Buck

   b. For Dr. Ken Mosely, loss is a "shattered dream."
      Define the dream that, for you, was shattered, lost.
      (The illusion, fantasy, the projection into the future)
      Offer time for sharing, if anyone wants to. This information often feels too "private."

5. Closure
   Probably most of us define and re-define our belief system. Our beliefs are often different at different periods of our lives. During or after a profound, life-shaking event we ask ourselves, what is the purpose or meaning of this? Does this event change my beliefs and, if so, how? And how will a change affect how I live my life? Let it help you to know we can struggle with these big questions together. You are not alone.

Steps to Meaning-Making

Goal: To transform the static event of "identity crisis" into the fluid patterns of "identity process."

Process = the willingness to *not* have everything neatly defined and settled "once and for all."

- **The establishment of a holding environment**

  honor/respect   creation/construction   confirmation   self/other's support

- **Data gathering**

  experience & understand aspects of self previously unknown or repressed
      (e.g. pattern of dependence...Why? Fear: of risk? failure? responsibility? standing
      out from the crowd? inadequacy? incompetence?
  creative questioning approach - compare and contrast
      personal present with past history
      one person's approach with another
      one opinion with another point of view
  entertain, perhaps try out, alternative styles or responses

- **Search for patterns & process**

  understanding old meanings in the creation of the new
  personal philosophies, mental structuring
  historical patterns of emotion, of image & ideal, of behavior, or responses to people &
      events

- **Nurture & encourage new or revived abilities**

  integrate and reconcile new insights with past history, understandings and experience
  new beginnings

Adapted from <u>Meaning - Making</u> by Mary Baird Carlsen, WW Norton, 1988.

LOSSES

We will mourn the loss of others. But we are also going to mourn the loss of ourselves - our identity as we knew ourselves, an earlier definition of our image of self.

Losses, however, have been lifelong. Necessary losses. The losses we confront by the inescapable fact. . .

> that our mother is going to leave us, and we will leave her;
>
> that our mother's love can never be ours alone;
>
> that what hurts us cannot always be kissed and made better;
>
> that we are essentially out here on our own;
>
> that we will have to accept - in other people and ourselves - the mingling of love with hate, of the good with the bad;
>
> that our options are limited by anatomy, mental and emotional expectations and assumptions;
>
> that there are flaws in every human connection;
>
> that our status on this planet is implacably impermanent;
>
> > and that we are utterly powerless to offer ourselves, or those we love, protection -- protection from danger and pain, from the roads of time, from the coming of death; protection from our necessary losses.

Adapted from <u>Necessary Losses</u>, Judith Viorst, 1988, Simon & Shuster, New York, NY.

I was amazed when I first learned a fascinating fact: that some of the stars in the sky are not there! We are seeing the light of stars that have already "nova"ed or imploded. They no longer exist. Scientists even remind us that our sun will last a long time, but that it too is dying and will one day be gone.

I bring home a dozen roses for the living room. A week later I notice that they are wilted and ready for the trash. I look in the mirror and notice a new wrinkle or a gray hair (if you have hair). Or. . . I have trouble walking one morning, I go to the doctor and find out that if I'm lucky I'll live two years -- and those two years won't be much fun.

Wherever I turn, the rug seems to be pulled out from under me. Is there nothing that will last forever? Is there no rock on which I can put my hope for the eternal? Is there no place I can rest my foot and say, "Ah, this won't move"?

I believe there is. Love will never die. The love I show to another will never be extinguished. Neither hate, persecution, indifference, nor pain can extinguish the love I have shown to another. If I have loved, I will live forever.

Source Unknown

119

no sooner than you are born
you are asked to die
to let go again
let go of it all
I weep
I mourn
I ache to the core
but I open my bonds
I let go
I stand like a rock
my strength WITHIN
                              -Tinka Taroa

Midway in our life's journey, I went astray from the straight
road and woke to find myself alone in a dark wood. How shall I
say what wood that was? I never saw so drear, so rank, so
arduous a wilderness. Its very memory gives shape to fear.
                              - Dante, *The Inferno*

...Creating a new theory is like destroying an old barn and erecting
a skyscraper in its place. It is rather like climbing a mountain,
gaining new and wider views, discovering unexpected connections
between our starting point and its rich environment. But the point
from which we started out still exists and can be seen, although it
appears smaller and forms a tiny part of our broad view gained by
the mastery of the obstacles on our adventurous way up.
                              - Albert Einstein

...Events that are apparently unconnected from one view become
interconnected when a broader view-point is taken... Theories
within theories - none of them the final truth at all.
                              - Jeremy Hayward

SESSION SEVEN

CLOSURES

Session 7: CLOSURES

What does it mean, to "say good-bye"?
How do I say it?

(Hold copies of "Absence" (p.125) from hand-outs, to be distributed after reading.)

1.   Overview

"Letting go" or "good-bye" has a feeling of finality, a feeling of closing the door; in
        French, au revoir = until I see you again
Good-bye is really only a contraction of "God be with you"
It is closure to one mode of relationship, but opening to another; the outward signs
        will become less important, but the inner connection, the legacy of heart,
        mind and spirit will remain strong and active. You can access it whenever
        you want.
Tell "Water Bugs" story. (p.124).
Read "Absence" (p.125) (and then distribute copies).

Stay open and receptive, try not to set mental limits on your experience. The
connection often happens when we are least guarded.

2.   Check -in

For your check-in, tell us if you sense your loved person in a different mode or
another dimension. (e.g. dreams, a sense of "presence," a sense of his guidance,
etc.) Or just tell us how your week went.

3.   We have a "style" of saying good-bye.

In your experience of being a host/hostess, you know there are some people who
leave a party *without* saying good-bye, preferably out the back door. There are
others who come to you and say, "Thank you, it's been a great party, and I had a
wonderful evening" and *leave*. There is a third kind who lingers in the doorway
talking, talking and talking, unwilling or unable to break away and close the
evening. You can probably place yourself somewhere in that range.

Steps/levels of closure:

Begins with the funeral or memorial service...giving away the clothes...
Distributing the personal possessions to family and friends...Doing the
paperwork...Perhaps moving...There will be many small closures and new
beginnings in the next months.

"I need you" is very different than "I love you and miss you." It is, I believe, the
secret of being able, or not able, to allow the loved person to leave. Anger and
resentment often reflect "I need you." Each of us has the potential for being
complete and whole within ourselves, but it is easier, we would often rather, have
our undeveloped side "carried" by the other person. It is hard work to access our
undeveloped potential. (There is a handout this week called "Developing your
opposite side," p.132)

4.   What were the gifts, what was the legacy your loved person left you?

        Guided imagery (pgs.126-127)
        Would anyone like to share his/her experience?

5.   Closure:

        This group is nearing completion, another ending for you.
        What are your options for further support?
                members from this group?
                another group?
                your own support system?
        Something I hope you learned here, and can transpose to your outside support
                system, is the bonding created by the sharing of feelings.
        This group was perhaps an initial step toward your healing. It was a first step
                toward taking responsibility, taking charge of your life.
        It perhaps represented a loosening of the preoccupation/grip of the past and "what
                was," to begin to focus on the present and the unknown, uncertain future.
        Next week we will make a date for a reunion.

"Water Bugs"

Down below the surface, in the mud at the bottom of a quiet pond, there lived a little colony of water bugs.

For many months they scurried busily around in the soft mud, but they did notice that every so often one of their colony seemed to lose interest in his friends. Clinging to the stem of a pond lily, he slowly climbed the stem, disappeared from sight and was seen no more; he did not return.

The water bugs wondered and were puzzled by this disappearance and made an agreement that the next one to climb the stem would promise to return and explain.

One day soon after their meeting, one of the water bugs found himself climbing up the lily stem, seeking the surface. Up, up, up he went, he broke through the surface of the water and rested on a lily pad. When he awoke, he was amazed to discover that he had gone through a wonderful transformation. A startling change had come over his body. His movement revealed four silver wings and a long tail. He felt the impulse to move his wings and, as the sun soon dried them, he suddenly found himself flying. He had become a dragonfly.

As he came back to rest on a lily pad, he looked down and saw he was right above his old friends, the water bugs, and remembered his promise. Flying back and forth above the water, peering down at his friends, he was dismayed to find that he could no longer enter the water. And even if he could, he realized that they would not recognize him in his new body. He would have to wait until they too become dragonflies.

Adapted from "Water Bugs and Dragonflies" by Dories Stickney

A B S E N C E

A Medieval Arabic Poem

I searched the sky
What if by chance
I find up there
A star you see

Travelers pass
What if I ask
If one of them
Inhaled your fragrance

Wind on my face
I feel what if
By chance it might
Bring news of you

On roads I drift
Hearing song on song
What if by chance
One breathed your name

Face after face I meet
Only to look away
What if in one I see
Your beauty's trace

-Abu Bakr al-Turtusi

Guided Imagery

In the midst of activity
Soft, slow breathing
Sets a balance.
An inward stillness
Becomes present.
The center point within us
Establishes itself.

For each of us it is so.
A center point within
Forms itself.
A center point is present
Not in space
But in our being.

A center point within us,
Our whole attention
At that center point
Present there in the stillness .
In the stillness of the Self

Through this center point
We move inward,
Inward and downward
Through a single straight shaft.
It is as though we go
Deep into the earth,
But within our Self.
Through the center point within.

We go inward,
Deeper,
Deeper inward.
Life is like the shaft of a well.
We go deep into it.
The life of each of us
Is a well.
Its sources are deep,
But it gives water on the surface.
Now, we go inward,
Moving through our center point,
Deeply inward to explore
The infinities of our well

Long enough
We have been on the surface
Of our life.
Now we go inward,
Moving through our center point
Inward,
Into the well of our self,
Deeply,
Further inward
Into the well of our Self

We move away
From the surface of things.
We leave
The circle of our thoughts,
Our habits, customs.
All the shoulds
And the oughts
Of our life
We leave behind.

We leave them on the surface
While we go inward,
Into the depths of our life.

Guided Imagery

From this center point deep within us, we look at loss.
Although there are many, we will choose one (or two) to focus on.
First the physical loss of a loved person from your life.
Second, a loss within.
Looking at these losses one at a time.

The art of bringing resolution is the way to evoke transformation and to produce meaning. You are experiencing the same process that all great ceremonies, rites of passage or vision quests explore - that of discovery of meaning with change, loss and transition.

1. Bring the loved person into your focus and hold him/her for a while within the still, quiet center...From this knowing, experience the memory of that person's spirit... Remember his/her personality as you knew it and let a quality emerge that is most significant for you... See the gift of that quality as she/he now holds it out to you... Wonder at what it might mean...Use all your senses to energize the experience of the gifting (see, hear, smell, taste, touch). Don't worry if you have yet to fully understand the gift; just try to hold it within. It is a symbol of the gift of the relationship, now changed... Find a way within to thank the giver of the gift and express your gratefulness...

2. Now, still holding your first gift, focus on the coming changes within you...Experience the memories and feelings that come up for you around change and transition...In bringing resolution, the old is related to the new; any death becomes the evoker of new life...choice joins fate to produce destiny. The wound and its healing are brought into new unity. Be aware of all the gifts of change that our experiences are giving us...Let all the mixture of thoughts and feelings be there... and allow yourself to focus in on one particular inner change that is coming up for you... See as a gift that quality of change as you now experience it...Wonder at what it might mean; use all your senses to energize the experience of the gift you have found within yourself...Hold it within and know it is a symbol of your inner gifts, now changing expression... Find a way within to thank yourself for finding this gift and express your gratefulness.

Then, in the time that is right for you, bring yourself and your gifts back to the room.

A Parable

I am standing upon the seashore. A ship at my side spreads her white sails into the morning breeze and starts for the blue ocean.

She is an object of beauty and strength. I stand and watch her until at length she's only a ribbon of white cloud just where the sea and sky come to mingle with each other.

Someone at my side says, "There, she's gone." Gone where? Gone from my sight, that is all. She is just as large in mast and hull and spar as when she left my side and just as able to bear her load of living freight to the place of destination.

Her diminished size is in me, not in her. And just at the moment when someone at my side says, "There, she's gone," there are other voices ready to send up the glad shout, "There, she has arrived."

And, that, my friends, is what dying is about.

Unknown Source

For Those I Love
For Those Who Love Me

When I am gone release me, let me go...
I have so many things to see and do,
You mustn't tie yourself to me with tears,
Be happy that we had so many years.

I gave you my love, you can only guess
How much you gave me in happiness.
I thank you for the love you each have shown,
But now it's time I traveled on alone!

So grieve a while for me, if grieve you must,
Then let your grief be comforted by trust.
It's only for a while that we must part,
So bless the memories that lie within your heart.

I won't be far away, for life goes on,
So if you need me, call and I will come.

Though you can't see or touch me I'll be near,
And if you listen with your heart you'll hear,
all my love around you soft and clear.
And then, when you must come this way
alone, I'll greet you with a smile and say,
"Welcome Home."

Anonymous

HOW NOT TO REGRET
REGRET

Dr. Richard Gotti
Empire State College

Regret is the pain people feel when they compare *what is* with *what might have been*. Regret is one of the most universal feelings. Our research has shown that men and women of all ages express regret about the results they feel from past actions.

TWO FACES OF REGRET

Regret is an inescapable part of life. For every choice we make, we give up a host of other options, leaving us open to feelings of regret. So, it's important to learn how to put regret into a livable context. If we are able to confront regret realistically, we can avoid its negative effects - and instead convert it into a positive tool to make effective life choices.

When regret over past events takes over people's lives, it leaves them stuck in the past...racked with self-blame...unable to make positive decisions. We are all familiar with fictional characters - and some in real life, too - who have never married because of one regretted romantic experience early on.

But regret can also serve a valuable *positive* function. Properly utilized, it can help us learn from our previous mistakes .... re-examine our personal values and goals in life...come to terms with the need to balance different aspects of our lives.

COMING TO TERMS WITH THE PAST

We all feel regret that something in our lives did not work out as it might have.

The degree of pain accompanying feelings of regret is closely related to the amount of self-blame we feel. But self blame over the past leads to depression in the present...and poor decisions in the future.

Coming to terms effectively with our regrets requires not self-blame but self-compassion. That does not mean excusing ourselves...just assessing the past realistically, and accepting our personal limitations.

Sometimes, external forces caused the situation that led to regret...people are seldom totally in control of a situation. While we can't change an event in the past, the one thing we *can* control is our attitude and reaction toward it in the present. Even if we did once make a really bad decision, we are not fated to continue on the same path forever. If we use our regret to understand what we did wrong, then we can hope to do better next time.

MAKING BETTER DECISIONS

Examining our regret can help us understand our true values and why our "real selves" are unhappy over what we did in the past.

It can build a bridge to a better future because understanding what we really want will make us better able to resist the external forces that caused our past mistakes...forces from family and friends or from the outside environment of beliefs and ideas that bombard us every day and persuade us unthinkingly to adopt wants and ambitions that we don't really share.

Understanding our true priorities in life is important because we suffer more regret *over the things we didn't do* than over the things that we did mistakenly.

Helpful: If we act in accordance with what we really believe, we are likely to suffer less regret later even if it doesn't work out the way we hoped. But if we never examine our priorities and just continue on the same path, afraid to take risks on a new endeavor lest we stumble, we are likely to end up with serious regrets over the roads not taken.

Regret can have a powerful effect on us. This is particularly true at certain times - birthdays, anniversaries, holidays - that focus our attention on differences between what was, what might have been...and what is.

HOW TO COPE WITH REGRET

There are a number of specific ways to harness regret as a help for making better future decisions, rather than a source of remorse or recrimination...

•**Altruism.** Do something positive for other people. Then you can feel genuinely good about yourself...and partly make up for past occasions when you may have wronged others. While women are traditionally attuned to caring activities, men also have much to gain by practicing their ability to help others.

•**Humor.** Past situations become easier to bear when we view them through the prism of humor. Regret is hardest to bear by people who regard themselves as perfect. Humor is a way to remind us that no one in the world, including ourselves, is perfect.

If you feel bad because of an embarrassing situation that you once experienced, exaggerate its most embarrassing features and imagine that they happened to a character in a comic movie. You'll be amazed how much better it makes you feel.

•**Seize the moment.** Try to live in the present. Make the most of every opportunity you are granted...to enjoy the company of family, new or old friends...to savor new experiences. Then, when the opportunity no longer exists, you'll feel much less regret over missing precious opportunities.

•**Surrender the need always to be right.** Don't confuse surrender with weakness. If you're willing to take the first step toward repairing a relationship - even if it bruises your ego a little now - you'll feel less regret and guilt later.

•**Reframing.** Shift your perspective in order to view a situation in a new light. Instead of thinking *I wasn't good enough for him/her,* shift to *What I had to offer wasn't appreciated.*

ANTICIPATE REGRET

The best way to avoid future regret is to think *now* about how today's decisions are likely to affect anticipated future situations. The better your decision, the less regret you're likely to feel.

When you know that a significant event is likely to occur in your life, begin thinking ahead about what you need to do - now and later - to prepare for it.

Even an apparently simple decision may have hidden consequences. So gather information...talk to others who faced similar choices...learn what their regrets were...try to get an objective view by hearing different perspectives.

Then, after weighing all the evidence, think about the prospective gains and losses...to yourself and others closest to you...about how you and they are likely to feel about it later. You'll be able to make a thoughtful choice that will minimize your future reasons for regret.

Gotti, Richard, "How Not to Regret Regret," <u>Bottom Line/Personal</u>., Reprinted with permission, Baoardroom Reports, New York, NY.

DEVELOPING YOUR OPPOSITE SIDE

It was Carl Jung's theory that every man has a feminine side and every woman a masculine aspect. Losing a mate/partner is a devastating experience and, possibly the partner fulfilled or "carried" the other side of your nature.

The following exercise might be helpful as you grow through this loss.

1. Think about several household jobs your partner took care of on a regular basis. Can you do these jobs yourself?

2. Think about several attributes you most admired about your partner. Are these attributes you could incorporate into your own personality?

3. Think about several activities your partner enjoyed. Would you be interested in carrying on one or more of these interests?

Embrace what you loved most; make it part of yourself...
That part of your loved one can live on in you.

GAINING PERSPECTIVE

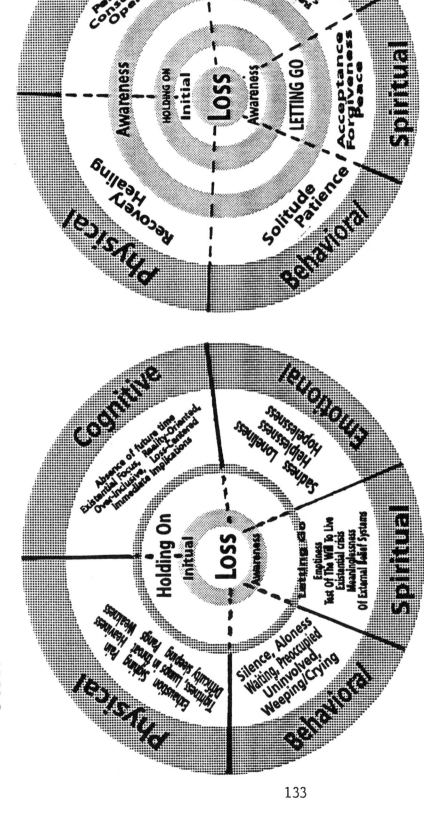

Cognitive
Perspective
Consequences
Openness

Emotional
Remembrance
Sweet Sadness
Vulnerability
softening of feelings

Initial
HOLDING ON
Awareness

Loss

Awareness
LETTING GO

Acceptance
Forgiveness
Peace

Spiritual

Solitude
Patience

Behavioral

Recovery
Healing

Physical

GAINING PERSPECTIVE

Grief process terminates in 3 different ways:
1. Return to strategies to limit awareness. Lack of defensiveness, coping strategies, struggle. (Incomplete grief)
2. Process of healing and acceptance. Live in present moment. Resignation, passivity
3. Builds on and includes healing/acceptance. Loss of motivation for change and growth. Reinvestment of energies elsewhere.

AWARENESS OF LOSS

Cognitive
Absence of future time
Existential Focus; Reality-Oriented.
Over-Inclusive; Loss-Centered
Immediate Implications

Emotional
Sadness Loneliness
Helplessness
Hopelessness

Initial
Holding On
Awareness

Loss

Awareness
Emptiness
Test Of The Will To Live
Existential crisis
Meaninglessness
Of External Belief Systems

Spiritual

Silence, Aloness
Waiting, Preoccupied
Uninvolved,
Weeping/Crying

Behavioral

Exhaustion Pain
Sighing Lumps in throat
Tightness Heaviness
Difficulty sleeping Pangs
Weakness

Physical

AWARENESS OF LOSS
FACING REALITY AND ITS IMPLICATIONS

Real awareness of the loss occurs in the absence of "coping strategies", ways of avoiding the loss are exhausted.
The experience of helplessness, deprivation, hopelessness, realization of own mortality. Challenge to will to live, physical stamina, emotional depth, search for meaning.
"I am exhausted, helpless, there seems to be

133

Loss as Possible Renewal
Bereavement: A Time of Transition
By Anne C. Grant, Ph. D.

At no time are we as open to healing and transformation as we are after a traumatic experience like a significant loss. It is only by a search for our inner resources that we probe their depths.

Grief is multidimensional. It is experienced on all levels of the personality: in the heart (feelings and emotions), the mind (thoughts), the spirit (meaning of life) and the body (the physical manifestations). All levels need our nurture, compassion and patience.

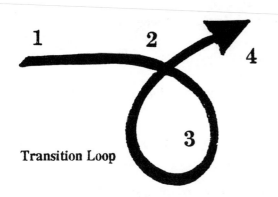

Transition Loop

Grief is a time of transition. The time begins (1) with the period between diagnosis and death. It is the shock, first, of anticipated loss, steps of trying to "prepare," of many smaller losses along the way: inability to drive the car, reliance on the walker or wheel chair, the hospital bed, the patient's world shrinking.

After the death, the second phase follows, (2) the numbness, not able yet to feel the awful weight of the new reality, perhaps denial.

The third (3) phase has the potential for transformation. It is a period of suffering: darkness, despair, flatness, emptiness, doubt, "limbo," withdrawal, preoccupation, a gap in life's continuity, the suspension of the loss of "what was" and is no longer, a time for many questions and few answers. Not understanding the "territory" or the goal, with no mental "map" to get from "here" to "there," the hallmark of this phase is confusion. An "in-between time," it gives the psyche time to rebuild, rearrange, recreate, re-configure itself, perhaps not understanding, without trying to know too soon, too fast. It is an encounter with our own death: the inner death of what was and the new which has not yet been formed. It is a time for balance between pushing/resting, between doing/allowing, effort/non-effort, compulsion/patience.

The fourth (4) step of a transition is a new beginning, identity and life in a newly integrated way, different from the past without abandoning the learnings, richness and the cherished memories. There is often growth and transformation after the loss of a loved one, but there is also the pain, anguish, stress, and the hard work of grief.

SUGGESTIONS FOR PROCESS

Grief is a **process,** not a state. Much pain results from being stuck in a state. The purpose of process is **movement through** the transition.

1. Allow yourself to feel the pain in increments you can bear. Perhaps, set aside a half hour, by the clock and, at its end, allow yourself distraction.

2. Be aware of your own unique needs and find people or places to accommodate their expression. Talking facilitates process. This is why it feels so compelling.

3. People who also knew and loved your lost person are perhaps the most satisfying. The person becomes alive between you as you share reminiscences.

4. In a time of intense vulnerability:
    * be as patient, gentle, compassionate and loving with yourself as you would like others to be with you;
    * Identify, acknowledge and then respect and honor your unique needs;
    * Learn to listen and trust your own inner voice;
    * Recognize that your feelings are more easily hurt in this time, so include in your life those people with whom you feel most safe.

5. Know that the process of grief will change you whether or not you want change. You cannot prevent it by fighting, stifling or concealing your feelings.

6. A major loss which cannot be ignored often triggers earlier minor losses which were not resolved at the time, making the present one seem even more overwhelming. Allow them to enter this current process.

7. Allow your "grief vocabulary" to evolve from statements of fact like "she's gone" or "he's dead" to statements which express your feelings, such as "I feel, I need, I wish, I miss."

8. Remember your grief process and your emotional "time line" are unique. Know that others are offering advice from **their** experience, which may not be appropriate or effective for you. It may be best to ignore them if they:
    * Tell you it doesn't do any good to talk about it;
    * Counsel you to be strong, not to focus on your pain and sadness;
    * Urge you to think of others who are worse off;
    * See your expression of sadness or despair as "wallowing";
    * Urge you to forget the past and get on with your life.

9. Though you may feel like withdrawing, remember that healing from loss is easier if you reach out to sources of support from friends, family, groups or organizations.

10. Funerals or memorial services are not the end of mourning, nor are they the only rituals which might serve your grief process. You might consider making your own collage of pictures to represent the relationship, or expressing your emotions visually by painting or drawing, verbally through poems, letters or a journal, musically through songs or recorded music, physically by interpretive dance, some form of body movement or a pilgrimage to a special place.

135

Understanding Sorrow

By Susan Lindstrom

SORROW (*Resistance*)

Sorrow is the tears you cry, and the ones you hide so that no one knows you are hurting inside.

Sorrow is the memory of life and regret of death.

Sorrow is the guilt and the self-condemnation for what was and what might have been.

Sorrow is the plans, expectations, and dreams shattered into little pieces.

Sorrow is the loneliness you feel inside even though you are surrounded by well-meaning friends.

Sorrow is the anger at our Creator for taking away someone so special.

Sorrow is the inner voice fighting with reality, trying desperately, even if in fantasy, to return to yesterday.

Sorrow is the automatic habits, triggers and sights heightening our senses, bringing with it the feeling of desperation.

Sorrow is confusion mixed with responsibility to make arrangements, stay in control, and let the loved one go; but continue with your own vacant life.

Sorrow is the doubt that life is worth all this pain and suffering.

Sorrow is the end of hope, the brick wall, the road to nowhere, the end of the line.

Or so we think, for beyond this valley is the road to understanding and acknowledgment.

UNDERSTANDING SORROW
Continued

UNDERSTANDING (Acknowledgment)

Understanding that the only thing you can count on in life is change.

Understanding that each moment is precious and is not to be wasted.

Understanding that loved ones are "loaned" to us and are not to be possessed; and when the time comes, in the physical life (as in divorce) or in the life beyond (as in death), we must let them go to their own individual destiny.

Understanding that there is life after death, and death after life, in an unending cycle, since the beginning of time.

Understanding that love transcends all time and space, keeping those dear to us connected from within.

Understanding that sorrow is the medicine upon the wounded heart, calling forth the natural antibodies of life to combat the infection of negativity and disease.

Understanding that how you feel about death is based on your present "perception" of it. This perception can be changed by acceptance of new beliefs.

Understanding that death is not "bad," but yet a new birth into something wondrous. The death of a caterpillar is the birth of a butterfly; the death of a seed is the birth of a flower; and the death of a loved one means only that the form has changed, but the life goes on to something different.

Be joyous in your own way for this new beginning. Let the memory nourish life and not death; let the love and energy derived from this relationship open your faith, not fear.

The Lord moves in mysterious ways, sometimes beyond our present comprehension. Out of the rubble comes order, and out of sorrow will come understanding and acceptance. Be grateful for that which you did have and not bitter for that which you did not.

Bereavement Magazine, September, 1989. Reprinted with permission, Bereavement Publishing, Colorado Springs, Co.

TOGETHER

Death is nothing at all. I have slipped away into the next room.

Whatever we were to each other, we still are. Call me by my old familiar name. Speak to me in the same easy way you always have. Laugh as we always laughed at the little jokes we enjoyed together. Play, smile, think of me, pray for me.

Life means all that it ever meant. It is the same as it always was. There is absolute unbroken continuity. Why should I be out of your mind because I am out of your sight? I am waiting for you, for an interval, somewhere very near, just around the corner.

All is well. Nothing is past. Nothing has been lost. One brief moment and all will be as it was before - only better. Infinitely happier. We will be one together forever.

Anonymous

GOAL SETTING TIME
How to set your life goals and attain them too
Amy E. Dean

Goals are simply changes you want to make in your life. They can be large (going to law school)..or small (making a phone call to keep up a friendship)...external (I'd like to double my salary in five years)...or internal (I'd like to feel more comfortable with myself).

Goals are the building blocks that make fantasies come true, turn dreams into reality. Goals give direction to our lives, but the process will *not* make our lives perfect or problem-free.

For goal-setting, we must pay attention to all major areas of life:
Emotions
- Access & appropriate expression
- Relationships
- Self-esteem

Mind
- Communication
- Career/lifework
- Stimulation

Spirit
- Appreciation of nature
- Faith/belief in a power greater than yourself
- Faith/belief in an overall structure that gives purpose to life
- Intuition or sensitive perception of the world around you, that helps you feel connected to the rest of the world

Body
- Health & fitness
- Balance of action/relaxation, doing/being, alone/with others

STEPS

- **Role Model:** An image of the person you would like to be - or the life you'd like to have - once you achieve your goal. Your role model might be a famous person, a character in a novel or a mental vision of yourself with qualities you'd like to achieve.

- **Mission:** A simple statement of what you want - your motivating desire. Example: I'd like to live in a house by the ocean.

- **Emotional Core:** What the goal means to you. Example: Having my own house would give me a sense of rootedness. Being by the ocean makes me feel centered and at peace.

139

•**Commitment:** The element that helps you distinguish between goals you set for yourself and goals you set to please others:

How badly do I want to achieve my goal?
Am I willing to work for it?

•**Guidelines:** The action plan that will help you reach your goal. Be as specific as possible.

•**Focus:** Gathering information and resources.

•**Timetable:** A realistic and flexible target date for accomplishing each goal.

•**Assessment/achievement:** A review of your progress. Simple and immediate goals give you immediate feedback. For longer-term goals, assess your game plan every few weeks or months.

•**Flexibility:** Being able to change on a set goal. There's nothing wrong with changing a goal 30 seconds after you set it, or even three years later. You may find the steps you've been taking are ineffective and you need to adopt a new strategy. Your time-frame may be too ambitious and require revision. Or changes in yourself or your life circumstances may have made the goal less valid - perhaps you need to drop it and set a new one.

•**Reward:** Taking time to appreciate yourself whenever you achieve a goal, no matter how small.

Dean, Amy E., "Goal Setting time," Bottom Line/Personal, Reprinted with permission Boardroom Reports, Inc., New York, NY.

Fundamental Skills for Living Life Well

Fortunately, our education doesn't end just because we left school. Life itself can be a classroom, our teachers are everything that happens to us, both positive and negative. In addition, each of us has our own Master teacher - that voice inside us that seems to be making calm, sure comments in the midst of mental chaos, directing in the midst of confusion, inertia or resistance - the still, small voice.

Our school teachers meant well, but they drilled into us huge quantities of information that we promptly forgot...and neglected to teach us some of the most fundamental skills for living well.

What they don't teach in even the best schools: Key things they left out:

What do you think is the *purpose* of your life? Why are we here?
>   We can't know for sure if there's a meaning to life, but *assuming* there is a responsibility for personal evolution, the fronts would be:
>   doing/learning
>   being/becoming
>   enjoying
>   lessons to be learned even from confusion & pain - learning is enjoyable, even if the events themselves are not

Do you think *forgiveness* is important? Why or why not?
>   Nursing a grievance may make us feel righteous, but it does not make us feel happy. When you forgive someone, you give not only to that person, but to yourself. Instead of focusing on hurt, anger, betrayal, you open yourself to love, joy & adventure. When we judge others, we also judge ourselves for being judgmental. Deep down, we know that we're inhibiting our happiness.
>   Say to yourself: I forgive (name of person) for (perceived offense)
>   I forgive myself for judging (person) for (offense).

 In life's scheme, what does "*balance*" imply to you?
>   Another incorrect thing that school taught: "There's always a right answer." Life is one contradiction after another, and most contradictions are valid. (e.g. The 10 Commandments: "do not kill"). We need to be vigilant to sense when we should rest/when we should act/when we should be flexible/when we should stand firm...what we should accept/what we should change. When in doubt, consult your Master Teacher - that quietly confident & sensitive inner voice. Ask: What would a Master do? Then do it.

Do you value *self-discipline?* Why or why not?

If our job is to become as good as we can be, to develop to our greatest potential, to our greatest personal power:

Without discipline, we can't improve ourselves, or be competent, or delay gratification or assume responsibility.

Without discipline we can't find reality & truth...we never evolve from children into productive adults.

People often look to someone or something else to solve their problems. Being disciplined requires assuming responsibility. To solve a problem, we have to admit we *own* it.

Do you think *mistakes* are good ____ bad ____ useful ____ wasteful ____? Why?

One of the most destructive things we learned in school is that mistakes are "bad" and should be punished.

If you avoid mistakes, you avoid accomplishing or learning anything. There is no experimentation...no learning...and no growth.

It's by finding out what *doesn't* work that we learn what *does.*

James Joyce: "Mistakes are the portals of discovery."

What does it mean to *love yourself?* Do you know how?

Do you know how to figure out *what you want?* How?

Don't be ashamed of your desires. You can have *anything*...but not *everything* you want. You may have to give up some things you want less for things you want more. But you can't get what you want unless you know what it is.

What do you most want?

How are you going to go after and get it?

Adapted from "Fundamental Skills for Living Life Well," by Peter McWilliams & M. Scott Peck in Bottom Line/Personal, Boardroom Reports, Inc., New York, N.Y.

Do not stand by my grave and weep

I am not there, I do not sleep

I am a thousand winds that blow,

I am the diamond glints on snow.

I am the sun on ripened grain,

I am the gentle autumn rain.

When you awake in the morning's hush,

I am the swift uplifting rush of

Quiet birds in circled flight.

I am the stars that shine at night.

Do not stand by my grave and cry,

I am not there, I did not die

Abdee
Source Unknown

George Leonard

Mastery...
Quick-Fix Thinking
...And Us.

We live in a time of instant gratification. We're told to take this pill for fast relief, or go on that quick weight-loss diet or buy a lottery ticket and become a millionaire overnight. Yet our addiction to quick-fix thinking is leading us to social and personal disaster.

George Leonard, a pioneer in work to develop the human potential, is working now to push us all to abandon our continuing search for quick results...and return to a more natural rhythm of life. He is finding more and more that fulfillment comes through what he calls *mastery*, the process of savoring the doing. *We asked him more about his views...*

What do you mean by a natural rhythm of life?

Studies of learning curves show us that the course of learning anything, your knowledge increases a little...then plateaus for a while, then goes up and down again... and then hits another plateau, but at a higher level.

For people to gain control of their lives they must realize that they're on a path of endless learning and growth. There's no such thing as getting to the top and staying there without further effort.

What is the key to mastering something?

You have to return again and again to the discipline or task...and stick to your work even when you appear to be going nowhere.

Mastery requires doing the best you can to improve - without pushing yourself *too* hard. You have to be willing to stay on the plateau as long as necessary.

Example: I was fortunate in my middle years to have found the practice of aikido, a martial-arts discipline, very difficult and totally resistant to the art of the quick fix.

When I first started with aikido, I assumed that I would steadily improve, but after a year and a half of practice, I was forced to recognize that I was on a plateau of rather formidable proportions. I was shocked and disappointed, but somehow I managed to persevere.

After a few more exhilarating spurts and disappointing plateaus, I found myself thinking, *Oh good, another plateau. I can just stay on it and keep practicing and sooner or later there will be another spurt.* It was one of the warmest moments on my journey toward the black belt I eventually earned.

Most people see practice as being a burden. What's your approach to it?

Practice is a path. In Chinese, the word is *tao* and in Japanese, *do*. Practice is the road upon which you walk - your path in life.

The great sports figures of our time are masters of their practice - and they love to practice.

Example: Larry Bird, who, without a doubt, is one of the best basketball players, is not all that talented. He owes his success to regular, intense practice - which he loves to do.

We call law and medicine practices, but today that's rarely the case. Modern law today isn't so much a practice as a get-rich-quick vehicle - and you can't call medicine a practice if you hardly know your patients.

In your job, the road to mastery will provide promotions, money and opportunity to excel. But the key is loving your work and being willing to hang in there through the tough times.

Why is mastery so difficult for Americans?

Because of our soured values as a country. We used to learn values from the village elders, rituals, religion and the family. Today we learn values from television and other media, which teach us that the ideal rhythm of life is a series of climactic moments.

Examples: In a cake commercial, you'll see glowing, happy faces around the cake and a child blowing out the candles, but you won't see any of the work that goes into baking. Or you'll see young people relaxing after a bicycle race by drinking diet soda, but you won't see the effort that went into the race. Or on sitcoms, you see complicated social and psychological problems dramatized, then magnificently solved in 22 minutes.

Television has established a rhythm in our culture that values the climax above everything and believes one climax should follow another.

Trying to maintain the rhythm of life as a perpetual high leads to such tragedies as our drug epidemic. Cocaine is the ultimate quick fix.

Quick-fix thinking has pervaded our society at every level. Modern medicine attempts to solve almost every problem with a drug or operation. Modern business sacrifices long-term planning and development to produce quick profits. Education has gone into a sharp decline because no one has the patience to master difficult subjects such as math or foreign languages.

The quick weight loss diet is one of the best examples of the quick fix...and long term weight control is one of the best examples of mastery. To keep weight off you have to permanently change your life-style, not just go on some fad diet for a few months.

What are the most common pitfalls on the road to mastery?

- **Obsessive goal orientation.** The desire of most people for quick, sure and highly visible results is the deadliest enemy of mastery.
- **A conflicting way of life**. The traveler whose main path of mastery coincides with career and livelihood is fortunate. Others must find space and time outside of regular working hours for their practice. *Keys:* Be realistic about balancing job, family and path...enlist the support of family and friends. *How to find the time:* Stop watching TV.
- **Lack of instruction.** For mastering most skills, there's nothing better than being in the hands of a master teacher, either one-on-one, or in a small group. But there are also books, films, tapes and other good instruction available.

145

- **Vanity.** To learn something new of any significance, you have to be willing to look foolish. Even after years of practice you may still take pratfalls.
- **Inconsistency.** Consistency of practice is the mark of the master. *helpful:* Establish a regular time and place to practice. But if you should happen to miss a few sessions, don't use that as an excuse to quit.
- **Perfectionism.** We set such high standards for ourselves that neither we, nor anyone else, could ever meet them. We fail to realize that mastery is not about perfection. It's about a process, a journey.
- **Dead seriousness.** Without laughter, the rough and rocky places on the path might be too painful for us to bear. Humor not only helps to lighten your load, it also broadens your perspective.

Reprinted with permission
"Mastery. . . Quick-Fix Thinking. . . and Us," George Leonard, <u>Bottom Line/Personal</u>, Boardroom Reports, Inc., New York, NY

Sometimes
By Marcia Updyke

Sometimes,
Memories are like rain showers
Sprinkling down upon you
Catching you unaware.
And then they are gone,
Leaving you warm and refreshed.

Sometimes,
Memories are like thunderstorms
Beating down upon you,
Relentless in their downpour.
And then they will cease,
Leaving you tired and bruised.

Sometimes,
Memories are like shadows
Sneaking up behind you,
Following you around.
Then they disappear,
Leaving you sad and confused.

Sometimes,
Memories are like comforters
Surrounding you with warmth,
Luxuriously abundant.
And sometimes they stay,
Wrapping you in contentment.

Reprinted with Permission

Bereavement Publishing

Colorado Spring, CO

SESSION EIGHT

NEW BEGINNINGS

Session 8: New Beginnings
Where am I now?
How do I go on?

Make date and plan for a reunion approximately one month from this date. It can take place as a potluck at a member's house, in a restaurant, a picnic in the park, etc. It can be brunch, dinner, afternoon "tea," whatever fits the preferences of the group.

1. Overview:
   Look around our "healing circle" and notice how different each person looks from the first night here. And know that you also look just as different. Allow yourself your own pace in this healing process.

The goal of "recovery" or healing is to:

   Learn to live with your loss

   Adjust to your new life accordingly

How do you go on?

How do you redesign your future after a crisis has changed your life?
   a. Feel fully whatever you feel.
   b. Explore whatever options are available; either imagine them or try them.
   c. Be receptive to new possibilities or opportunities; try not to allow your mind to set limits on your potential experience.
   d. Live as fully as possible with the resources available in the present.
   e. Let go of whatever must be left behind. Your reality must reflect that, in spite of your intense wishes to the contrary, he is no longer physically there and will no longer be able to interact with you as he did in the past.
      If you think of the future in terms of the past, it allows no creativity. If you invent your future, not modeled on the past, you're free to act in different ways.

Imagine your two hands clasped together with intertwined fingers, almost as though they were folded in prayer. One hand represents you and the other, the one you love who has died. When two people love each other and are invested in each other, they are intertwined emotionally, they are bonded together as represented by your two hands. When one of the two dies, the remaining person has to relinquish the old attachments and develop new ones. To keep your hand positioned as though yours is still intertwined with another's, but to have no other hand there, renders your hand useless. Your remaining hand, now not supported by the other, must learn to move in new ways, to be free someday to clasp another hand or to do other things.

(Adapted from *Grieving* by Therese Rando)

2. Check-In
   Tell us where you are in the healing process.
   Or just tell us how your week went.

3. What Healing *will* mean:
   You can expect a changing identity, the redefining of roles, relationships and skills. These can either be positive or negative. You *do* have a choice over how you allow the loss to affect you.
   - Are you richer or diminished from having loved and lost?
   - Will you make the most of the rest of your life, perhaps as a living memorial to your loved one or will you be bitter and resentful?
   - Is loss the catalyst for growth or will you be stuck and never again take a risk?
   - Will you try never again to have unfinished business with loved ones or will you feel "the world owes me"?

4. Guided review
   Get comfortable in your chairs, close your eyes and take a few deep breaths while I take you on a brief review of where we have been in our evenings together.
   - We've talked about the continuum and uniqueness of what is normal for grief
   - We looked at trusting and caring for all aspects of ourselves: heart, mind, spirit and body. We acknowledged our own responsibility for this as well as expecting it from our support systems
   - We discussed the importance of recognizing and expressing feelings
   - We explored looking for life's meaning or purpose
   - We examined what it means to make closures
   - Probably most helpful of all has been the sharing of our own and each other's feelings
   Take time to reflect on any or all of these.
   What stands out for you?
   Allow a picture or symbol or sound to come to mind which represents how you experience yourself now. When you are ready, draw this picture.

   After each member has shared his/her picture, return the first evening's picture and compare. Usually there is a marked and noticeable difference between the two, allowing the member to visualize the leap in his/her process.

5. Closure
   Have ready a lined basket of sand and a short (votive) candle for each member (including yourself). Give each a candle, light the candle of the person on your left, who in turn lights the candle of the next person, etc. Have each put his/her candle in the sand.

   It looks like each of those flames has edges, boundaries, and yet notice how the light of each merges and blends with each of the others, making a fused glow. It is like that with us also. It appears that we each are bounded by our skins, that we are separate, yet we have experienced the fused glow from our combined spirits, the love and compassion and caring of each for all the others. Remember, and let it strengthen you as you continue on your journeys...

   See you at the reunion!

RECOVERING FROM GRIEF

Grief is a difficult and lengthy process. In the beginning you wonder if you will ever resolve it. You may wonder what life could be like beyond your grief. As the months go by, you may think you are getting nowhere. A visual record, like a journal or series of art works, might help you to see your progress; otherwise, change being so gradual, it is hard to see. It is like a wound that heals ever so slowly. As the pain diminishes, you forget how bad it used to be.

The signs of healing, which occur a little at a time:
    You begin to regain a focus on others:
        - become more interested in others' activities
        - have enough energy to get involved in what others are doing
        - notice the thoughts and feelings of others.
    You can live with your emotions:
        - your emotions are less intense and less volatile
        - you have learned to handle them safely
        - you can experience them, write about them, express them you yourself and
          others.
    You are able to laugh and enjoy yourself:
        - you have more frequent "good" days and fewer "bad" days
        - enjoy pleasurable moments
        - go several hours a day not thinking about your loss
        - you may feel guilty about feeling better - this will pass. It, in no way, diminishes
          the love or importance of relationship.
    You can talk about your loved one without crying or getting a lump in your throat.
    You can share your feelings with others without becoming overwhelmed by them.
    You can take pride in your courage, your accomplishments and your ability to take
        care of yourself. Your self-esteem is returning.
    You can think about your loved one, look at pictures, or go places which bring back
        memories without becoming mournful and sad.
    You find meaning in your life once again; a sense of purpose in your work, in
        relationships, in nature.
    You begin setting new goals.
    You start planning for the future:
            - plan vacations, holidays, gatherings with friends/family
            - plan those "special days" without dread or anxiety
    You are doing what is normal, natural, necessary; you are adjusting to life without
        your loved one, loosening the knots of the past.
    You are beginning to recreate, re-configure your identity, not in terms of the past, but
        with new understandings of meaning, options and directions.

Adapted : Source Unknown

Getting Better

By Janet Zinzeleta

During the first months after my husband's death, I remember hearing so often from others, "It gets better," and, "The first year is the hardest." I had the idea that somehow, after the first-year anniversary of his death, I would magically feel better.

My husband has been dead for three years now, and I still miss him a great deal. There are still days when memories wash over me, and I am as acutely overwhelmed with loss as I was at the beginning. When I say this to the newly widowed, they get a look of hurt surprise in their eyes and I think, "Oh dear, I shouldn't have said that." They want to hear that they won't always feel as badly as they do now; and it's true, they won't. But the process of healing is a slow and gradual one.

To me, the simile that best explains the situation is a comparison of the loss to a very bad wound, like a third degree burn, or severe laceration. The pain of the new injury is extreme; and often there is redness, bleeding or some other evidence of the seriousness of the trauma.

At first, the pain may be so bad that it is almost impossible to see the nearly imperceptible beginning of healing.

So it is with grief. As the days turn into months, one still marvels at the enormity of the hurt. But, if one is doing "grief work," that is, making an effort at recovery, the healing is beginning.

Just three months after my husband's death, I attended a workshop for widows. One of the members of the group was recounting how her husband had died, and as she did, the tears streamed down her cheeks.

The coordinator of the meeting asked gently, "How long has your husband been dead?"

"Four years," the woman replied.

I was aghast! Would I still feel that badly after four years?

As in the case of a physical wound, after healing, there will be a scar. The affected area will be sensitive and tender. Even a long time after the cut has healed, there can be a good deal of pain if it is bumped or disturbed. So, too, emotional "bumps" such as the anniversary of the death, wedding anniversaries, holidays, cause us pain.

How, then, do things get better? We begin to get distracted from the hurt by new things in our lives, and we begin to understand that there are aspects to life other than our grief, even though there may always be some pain. We get used to not having our loved one as an integral part of our daily lives.

At the beginning, we think of almost nothing but our loss, and we may experience the pain of longing and grief nearly every hour of the day. We may feel as if a heavy weight is in our chest. As time passes though, we gradually are able to divert our attention from the pain. When it hurts, it hurts just as badly as ever, but it hurts less often. Eventually, we are able to focus on things other than our grief - even enjoy them.

If we imagine how impossible this would have felt at the start, we can begin to acknowledge that eventually it does get better.

Berevement Magazine, Reprinted with permission Bereavement Publishing, Colorado Springs, CO.

Learning To Live with the Loss in Terms of Yourself

You have returned to your normal levels of psychological, social, and physical functioning in all realms of your life.

There is a general decline in all of your symptoms of grief

You are not overwhelmed by emotions in general or whenever the loss is mentioned.

You are back to your normal level of self-esteem.

You can enjoy yourself without feeling guilty, and you don't feel guilty for living.

Your hatred and anger, if any, doesn't consume you and is not directed inappropriately at others.

You do not have to restrict your emotions and thoughts to avoid confronting something painful.

It is not that you don't hurt, but the hurt now is limited, manageable, and understood.

You appreciate how you are similar to and different from other bereaved persons.

You do not have to obsess about nor think solely of the deceased and the death.

You feel that you have done what you needed to do, either to atone for your guilt or to learn to live with it.

You lead the pain, it doesn't lead you.

You can appreciate the bittersweet quality of certain experiences, such as holidays and special events in which you feel the sweetness of those who are around you as well as the sadness of not being with your deceased loved one.

Your are able to meet and cope with secondary losses in a healthy fashion.

You don't become unduly anxious when you have nothing to do . You don't have to be occupied all the time to be without tension.

You can remember without pain, and can talk about the deceased and the death without crying.

You no longer feel exhausted, burdened, or wound up all the time.

You can find some meaning in life.

You do not have to hold time, or yourself, back.

You have "accepted" the loss in the sense of not fighting the fact that it happened.

You are comfortable with your new identity and the new adjustments you have made to accommodate being without your loved one in the world. While you wouldn't have chosen to have to change, you are not fighting it now.

You are comfortable with the emotions that temporarily are aroused when you occasionally bump the scar from your loss (for example, at anniversaries or special events). You know how to deal with the grief and you understand that it is normal.

You know how and when to take time to mourn.

You can look forward to and make plans for the future.

You have a healthy perspective on what your grief resolution will and will not mean for you.

Learning to Live with the Loss in Terms
of Your Relationship with the Deceased

You can realistically remember the good and the bad, the happy and sad of both the deceased and your relationship.

Any identification you have with the deceased is healthy and appropriate.

You can forget the loss for a while without feeling like you are betraying your loved one.

You have a comfortable and healthy new relationship with the deceased, with appropriate withdrawal of emotional energy but also appropriate ways to keep that person "alive."

You are able to stop "searching" for your lost loved one.

You do not have to hold onto the pain to have a connection with your deceased loved one.

The rituals that keep you connected to your loved one are acceptable to you and healthy.

You can concentrate on something besides your deceased loved one.

In your relationship with your deceased loved one, you have achieved healthy amounts of holding on and letting go.

Learning to Live with the Loss in Terms
of Adjusting to the New World

You have integrated this loss into your ongoing life. You are able to relate to others in a healthy fashion and to work and function at the same level as before.

You can accept the help, support, and condolences of others.

You are not inappropriately closed down in your feelings, relationships, or approaches to life. For example, you do not overprotect yourself or fail to take any risks.

You can let the world go on now without feeling it has to stop because your loved one has died.

You can deal with others' insensitivity to your loss without becoming unduly distressed or overemotional.

You are regaining interest in people and things outside of yourself or which don't pertain to your lost loved one.

You can put the death in some perspective.

There may be other signs that would indicate to you that you now are learning to live with your loss in as healthy a fashion as possible. The ones listed here will give you some examples of the ways in which resolutions and recovery can be shown. You will note that none of them suggest that you not have some connection with your deceased loved one, or that you forget that person. They all center around learning to live with the fact of your loved one's absence, moving forward in the world despite the fact that the scar will remain and, on occasion, bring pain.

A Final Perspective

And, in the end, this moving forward with that scar is the very best that we could hope for. You would not want to forget your loved one, as if she had never existed or not been an important part of your life. Those things that are important to you in your life are remembered and kept in the very special places of your heart and mind. This is no less true with regard to the loss of a beloved person. Keep this loss, treasure what you have learned from it, take the memories that you have from the person and the relationship and, in a healthy fashion, remember what should be remembered, hold on to what should be retained, and let go of that which must be relinquished. And then, as you continue on to invest emotionally in other people, goals and pursuits, appropriately take your loved one with you, along with your new sense of self and new way of relating to the world, to enrich your present and future life without forgetting your important past.

From Grieving: <u>How to Go On Livig When Someone You Love Dies</u>, Reprinted with permission Theresa Rando, Macmillian Publishing Company, New York, New York, 1988.

Self-Care During Restructuring

In winter one has to accept not knowing and affirm life without results, affirm life in and of itself, and then comes spring when life buds and small green shoots appear. It would seem that this season spring would be easiest to accept, but we know that suicide rates are high in spring. If one hasn't related properly to winter, if one has fought it and not really accepted the possibility of both birth and death, or if one has gone into it too deeply, forgetting the passage of seasons, then one may not be able to accept the new and, fearing change, will cling to depressions and the old.

from: *The Wounded Woman* by Linda Leonard.

If we have lived through the falling apart, the breaking down of destructuring and the waiting, and the doubting and resting of the time in-between, the process will take us naturally to restructuring. Here, as Linda Leonard implies, with the first buds of spring, there are signs that the future is beginning to exist again. One begins to get glimpses of a new life, of the growing warmth of the sun, of buds that will be flowering, of curled leaves that will uncurl. Hope returns and begins too. What are the guidelines for self-care during this time?

One thing to be aware of after going through such a difficult time is that it is very natural to be so delighted when the new begins to appear that one grasps for it, seizes on it immediately. It is important to go slowly, stay open, receive the new, but not to close on it too fast, for it may be that what you are seeing is only one leaf of a larger branch, one part of a larger pattern. So do not be too hasty.

Do not settle too soon on what the new direction will be, but use the signs instead as a time of trial and error, of exploration. Test the waters, experiment, do not be afraid to make mistakes. Some of these new leaves may not be right for you, and yet those very mistakes may be essential in clarifying what your direction will be. This part of the process is like all the rest - a gradual one - though our tendency is, as always, to settle it too quickly.

It seems to be helpful to remember that we are working with the *re*-forming of a process that is deep inside us. We need to leave time to allow the new integration to take shape. It is a process that is deeper than our conscious mind can fathom. Something new is trying to reconstruct itself within us. We need to give it space and time. This does not mean waiting passively or limply, but being in a state of alert, aware receptivity.

I suppose the two polarities to be aware of are the need to be totally sure before acting, which tends to lead to passivity, inertness, and dependency, and the need to act quickly, to grasp at the new. Knowing our own propensities in these situations, we will know what to guard against.

On a practical level, this could be a time for reviewing the writing that has been done during the transition. As the new direction begins to become clear, it can be very helpful to see the order inherent in the whole process.

One of my clients, a man in his forties, going through what could be called a mid-life crisis, took one afternoon to re-read his journal and was amazed to see that this period, which had seemed do dark, so inchoate, so seemingly random, had an inner order. A thread had run throughout, yet in the moment, it had been impossible to see.

This kind of looking back strengthens one's faith in the process of growth and gives one new strength to go through difficulties and to stand steadily by those who are going through something similar. It brings a faith based on life's experience that is much deeper than any theory or any model of the human psyche.

by: Anne Yeomans
Reprinted with permission
an excerpt from "Self-Care During Dark Times"

What "Recovery" and Healing <u>May</u> Mean for You

Changed or new experiences and/or priorities

Increased awareness of life's preciousness/fragility/brevity, resulting in a positive, life-affirming and enhancing force

Increased commitment and unity with other loved ones

Increased compassion and caring toward others

Via pain transformed, perhaps heightened perceptions, raised state of consciousness, increased spirituality

Pain transformed via art, literature or music

Having faced the ultimate loss of death, perhaps becoming open without fear of vulnerability

Channeled pain or rage to assist others or society (e.g. political focus)

Discovery and/or development of new aspects of identity previously unknown or unused

What "Recovery" Will <u>Not</u> Mean

You will not forget, either your loved one or the "old" world

It does not mean that you will not have any relationship at all with your loved one

Recovery does not mean you are always happy, with never any more pain

It does not mean you will be untouched by certain reminders like a certain song, that particular smell, or that special location

It will not mean that you do not experience the bittersweet combination of feelings that holidays can bring, rejoicing with present loved ones and mourning those no longer here

It will not mean that in certain events in your life you do not painfully wish for your loved one to be alive and present with you, to share in your joy or be proud of you

Recovery will not mean that you don't mourn any longer, but rather that you learn to live with the mourning in ways that do not interfere with your ongoing healthy functioning in the new life without your loved one

The mourning will never cease entirely. Total resolution of mourning, in the sense of completely and permanently finishing it and never being touched again by some element of the loss, usually never truly occurs.

REMEMBER

Remember me when I am gone away,
Gone far away into the silent land;
When you can no more hold me by the hand,
Nor I half turn to go, yet turning stay.
Remember me when no more day by day
You tell me of our future that you plann'd.
Only remember me; you understand
It will be late to counsel then or pray.

Yet if you should forget me for a while
And afterwards remember, do not grieve;
For if the darkness and corruption leave
A vestige of the thoughts that once I had,
Better by far you should forget and smile
Than that you should remember and be sad.

Christina Rossetti

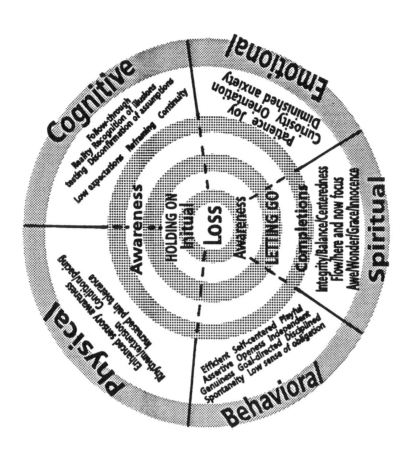

REFORMULATING LOSS

Usually occurs after some type of resolution. Energy freed is available for new self-awareness.

Motivation is often recognition of life's finiteness.

Perceptual changes:

focus on limits ⟶ potential

              problems ⟶ challenges

              coping ⟶ growth

Reformulation extends self-trust & self awareness.

As long as loss is seen only as tragic, limiting, or the end of life, then growth cannot emerge from grief.

Loss reformulated in terms of possibilities, opportunities

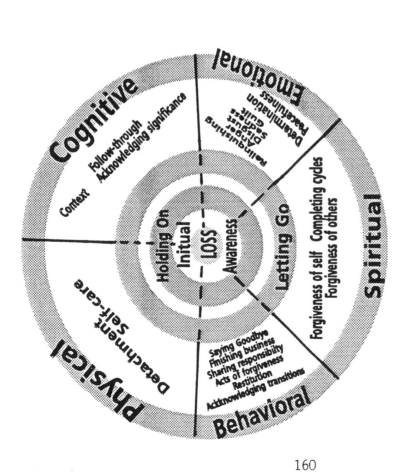

RESOLVING THE LOSS

The purpose of this phase is to allow opportunities to detach from aspects of life now over or having no longer current meaning or function.

Often people do not go past the phase of "gaining perspective."

1. If they have chosen to limit awareness, chance to be freed from grief itself is also limited.

2. If they have chosen acceptance, it may reflect a passive, often resigned step for facing the inevitable.

3. Acknowledgement in a shared way that what is past is over, frees energy from investment in the past and allows

Transforming Loss

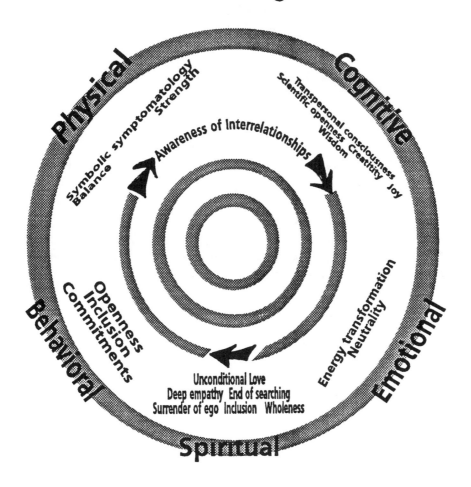

Involves placing the loss in a context of growth, life cycles and the perception that grief is a unifying rather than alienating experience.

The loss frequently seen as an alteration of the nature of the relationship rather than a complete, utter severing or discontinuity.

Because growth from grief is not by choice, such growth is a gift. Against their will, their rational, logical sense, the loss they wish hadn't happened comes an even deeper sense of aliveness, self awareness, and growth.

Integration.

Reinvestment in the outside world, rediscovery of social self.

Expression of meaning (search has ended)

Awareness of interrelationships.

Strength as capacity to integrate energies from many sources.

Balance of self aspects.

Trust in self wisdom.

Openness to major shifts in life-style & ways of experiencing the world.

Transformation & expression of freed energy.

161

RULES FOR BEING HUMAN

1. **You will receive a body.**

   You may like it or hate it, but it will be yours for the entire period this time around.

2. **You will learn lessons.**

   You are enrolled in a full-time informal school called life. Each day in this school you will have the opportunity to learn lessons. You may like the lessons or think them irrelevant and stupid.

3. **There are no mistakes, only lessons.**

   Growth is a process of trial and error, experimentation. The 'failed' experiments are as much a part of the process as the experiment that ultimately 'works.'

4. **A lesson is repeated until learned.**

   A lesson will be presented to you in various forms until you have learned it. When you have learned it, you can then go on to the next lesson.

5. **Learning lessons does not end.**

   There is no part of life that does not contain its lessons. If you are alive, there are lessons to be learned.

6. **"There' is no better than "here."**

   When your 'there' has become a 'here' you will simply obtain another 'there' that will, again, look better than 'here.'

7. **Others are merely mirrors of you.**

   You cannot love or hate something about another person unless it reflects to you something you love or hate about yourself.

8. **What you make of your life is up to you.**

   You have all the tools and resources you need. What you do with them is up to you. The choice is yours.

9. **Your answers lie inside you.**

   The answers to life's questions lie inside you. All you need to do is look, listen and trust.

10. **You will forget all this.**

...Anonymous

When I'm feeling. . .

        guilty
        crazy
        lonely
        scared
        disoriented
        forgetful
        overwhelmed

And I feel I have. . .

        no motivation
        no appetite
        no interests

Or that I should. . .

        be dealing with this better
        pull myself together
        not burden my friends

When I. . .

        can't sleep
        don't breathe normally
        catch cold easily
        worry about my future
        am obsessed with my loss

        I can turn this page and tell myself...

I am doing as well as I can for today.

I will take good care of myself.

I have the strength to face my grief.

I can take as long as I need to heal myself.

I can cry if I need to.

I have the courage to live alone.

I did the best I could for my loved one.

I will "get on with my life" when I am ready.

I will take one day at a time.

I am stronger and have more inner resources than I think.

I will heal and recover.

Source Unknown

SUGGESTED READINGS

SUGGESTED READINGS

Bouvard, Marguerite, *The Path Through Grief*, Brewer Press, Wellesley, MA.

Colgrove, Bloomfield, McWilliams, *How To Survive the Loss of a Love*, Prelude Press, Los Angeles, CA.

Ericsson, Stephanie, *Companion Through The Darkness*, Harper Collins, New York, NY.

Fumia, Molly, *Safe Passage*, Conari Press, Berkeley, CA.

James, J., Cherry, F., *The Grief Recovery Handbook*, Harper & Row, New York, NY.

McKay, M., Rogers, J., *When Anger Hurts*, New Harbinger Publications, Oakland, CA.

Rando, Therese A., *Grieving: How to go on Living When Someone You Love Dies,* Macmillan Publishing Company, New York, NY.

Schneider, John, Stress, *Loss and Grief*, Aspen Publishers, Inc., Gaithersburg, MD.

Staudacher, *Carol, Men & Grief*, New Harbinger Publications, Inc., Oakland, CA.

Viorst, Judith, *Necessary Losses*, Simon & Schuster, New York, NY.

FACILITATOR NOTES